X 30

THE GOLFERS

The Golfers–
THE INSIDE STORY

By Members of
the Association of Golf Writers

Edited by Peter Dobereiner
Foreword by Henry Cotton

COLLINS
St James's Place, London   1982

William Collins Sons & Co. Ltd
London · Glasgow · Sydney · Auckland
Toronto · Johannesburg

British Library Cataloguing in Publication Data

The Golfers.
  1. Golf—History—Addresses, essays, lectures
  I. Dobereiner, Peter
  796.352′09   GV963
  ISBN 0-00-216385-3

First published 1982
© Peter Dobereiner 1982

Photoset in Garamond
Made and Printed in Great Britain by
William Collins Sons & Co. Ltd, Glasgow

ACKNOWLEDGEMENTS

Most of the contributions in this book were written specially for it. In certain cases the authors submitted previously published work, and grateful acknowledgement is due to the original sources for permission to reprint, specifically: *Financial Times, Golf Digest, Glasgow Herald, Golf World, The Guardian, Golf Monthly, Country Life*, Cassell and Company (for the extract from Henry Longhurst's autobiography *My Life and Soft Times*), *Sunday Tribune, Yorkshire Post, Irish Times*.

I would also like to express my thanks to the unsung heroes who did the hard graft of typing the manuscript and, above all, to the writers, both for their contributions and for their enthusiasm and encouragement which sustained me in my labours when I would much rather have been out playing golf.

PETER DOBEREINER

CONTENTS

FOREWORD

HENRY COTTON
Vice-President of the Association of Golf Writers

My earliest book of newspaper and magazine cuttings, started by my father, shows that even in the 1921 Boys Championship I was noticed by the Press and, as I developed, my golf became news. Those who wrote the pieces became friends. Now most of them who knew me in my prime, twenty to forty years ago, have long gone, maybe to report better tournaments on better courses, as I hope, and new writers have succeeded them on earth.

Henry Longhurst was a lifelong, loyal friend and he, too, has now gone after a long and painful illness, even though he kept on with his writing and TV commentating to the end. He made a worldwide reputation as a commentator, with his wit and well-timed pauses. He finally put his clubs away in the attic when he acquired the cursed twitch on the greens. I liked that defiant gesture.

Interviews in pre-war days were conducted in the locker room, or in one's car, and as the players were usually thirsty and tired they were often done hurriedly by the golf writers, standing uncomfortably between the lockers with every passer-by jogging their elbows. Now there is an interview tent to which the player is delivered by buggy, to a special seat on a raised platform, microphone, and any desired drink is delivered to his hand, and the Press – hundreds of them for the Open – sit more or less comfortably on plastic chairs with writing pads on their knees. In the press tent today there are private telephones, typewriters on baize-covered tables in front of a huge board carrying hole by hole scores of every competitor.

I wonder what my long-departed golf-writing friends, who had to scramble around the course with the crowds following one pair of players, would have thought of today's arrangements.

There were fewer tournaments then, of course. Now there is one a week over a long season. The life is not very glamorous, and it is exhausting to travel thousands of miles following golf, living out of a suitcase and watching the same circus acts perform week after week. Yet they get on well together. To be with them, and to share their gaiety and wit, is a tonic. And what loyal friends they are too.

My advice to every young golfer is to make friends with the boys of the pen. They nearly all play the game and know what golf is about, and never miss a chance to play a few holes if there is a course nearby. There is quite a bit of golfing rivalry among them, too.

I am proud to number many of the golf writers among my personal best friends and appreciate their suffering when they lose a bet to me on the course. Then the roles are reversed and I am the interviewer saying 'Bad luck'.

Toots and I look forward to our regular get-togethers with our golf-writing friends. They may be boozy, or bawdy or blasphemous at times but, by golly, they are never dull. The same goes for this book, which consists of contributions from members of the AGW. Collectively the writers represent more than a thousand years of experience of golf in all its facets and in this book you will find revelations, wisdom and wit. The one element you will not find is scandal. What a book they could write if they were so minded but they have a code as strict as any religious order and everyone knows, golfers and writers, when the notebooks are open and when they are shut. Fleet Street may have its muck rakers but the golf writers are not among them. Their job is to be the eyes and ears of the newspaper reading public and since I have now joined the ranks of those millions who must keep in touch with this great game of golf mainly through reading their reports, I appreciate how acute their hearing is, how perceptive their vision. After reading this book I think you will appreciate it too.

PART ONE

You should have been there

Into the lioness's den

PETER RYDE

The dark-haired tomboy of a foreigner sat alone munching her cornflakes and reading the local papers. The coming of the US Women's Open Championship to the Virginia Hot Springs club was splashed all over their sports pages. Form was studied in detail. But of the arrival of the French amateur who had the effrontery to challenge the supremacy of America's best professionals, no mention was made. Even if they had known of her arrival they would still have ignored her. After all, no amateur had ever won the title, no foreigner had ever won it, nor had anyone won it as young as this Catherine Lacoste who had just celebrated her twenty-second birthday in that summer of 1967. The idea was unthinkable.

Miss Lacoste might not have existed. This only steeled her ambition. Forty years before, her father, René Lacoste, had crossed the Atlantic and won the US Singles Tennis Championship. Forty years before, her mother, as Mademoiselle Thion de la Chaume, had crossed the English Channel and won the British Women's Open Golf Championship. They had offered to accompany her on this trip; Catherine would not hear of it. They had achieved their victories alone; she wished to do the same, thereby stepping out of their shadow into her own limelight.

She was, in truth, not quite alone. At the next table to hers sat Mr and Mrs William C. Preston from Charlottesville and their two daughters. Such was the parents' interest in golf that they had booked out of the hotel on the first day of the championship. Catherine's magnetic way with children has become something of a legend. Something about her directness of manner and her teasing vitality immediately attracts them. Lesley and Cathy fell under her spell and implored their parents to stay just one more day. Miss Lacoste scored an opening seventy-one, tied second, one stroke behind Sandra Haynie.

When the second day broke the local press had perforce to take note. There were zany headlines: 'The Murderous Mademoiselle', 'De Gaulle's Secret Weapon'. The American writers had been caught napping, but they are no fools and the epithets they used about her were on target. Bubbling, friendly, speaking better English than they.

They were not exaggerating. Her English was fluent, even voluble: but more important, probably no woman in the world has ever hit a one-iron as she could. And in one respect she had the edge on the American professionals. Because golf was not her source of livelihood she had never learned the percentage shot. Her game was attack, attack, all the way.

Second day. Catherine checks the mascots in her handbag – the little green felt crocodile, symbol of the family Lacoste which world-wide merchandizing has since made famous, a miniature cat, and a little rag-doll which she had made herself five years before. She scored seventy and her half-way total of 141 led the field by five from Margie Masters of Australia and Suzie Maxwell. She played that day with inspiration and boundless confidence. '*Je n'ai jamais connu un tel état de grâce*,' was her untranslatable comment on it. Return of the Prestons to Charlottesville indefinitely postponed. Telephone call from the French Ambassador in Washington: 'You are a better ambassador than I, Mademoiselle.' Telephone to Le Crocodile in Paris, the only coach she ever listened to: 'But I told you before you left that you had a good chance, *ma petite fille*; you are going to win!'

Sandra Haynie, deposed as tournament leader, thought so too.

Another great golfer, Patty Berg, described her as possessing the most complete personality she had ever come across. 'She laughs and cries like a youngster of sixteen, but she plays golf like a veteran trooper.' Not all the professionals were so generous. Many thought, or hoped, that she would succumb; if she did not they were going to lose $5000 and a whole lot of prestige.

Catherine withstood the third-round pressure, and although she took forty to the turn by the end of the day she had retained her five-stroke lead. It was not until the final round that the cracks began to appear, and at the seventeenth her lead was down to one with a pack of the best women golfers in the world on her heels. She survived because she was aware that for her there was another world waiting beyond the winning of championships. Also there was the blood of champions in those veins.

On the seventeenth tee she gathered her courage and cut the corner of the dog-leg, her ball sailing over the tree tops – a calculated risk no professional would have taken, but it came off. A ten-foot putt for a birdie there and she had given herself the two-stroke cushion she needed to face the ordeal of the final hole. And who is that perched on her shoulders now as she performs a lap of honour at the conclusion of the prize-giving ceremony? No other than little Cathy Preston, with whose father later that evening in the ballroom Catherine flung herself barefoot into a frenzied Charleston.

How wrong can you be!

CHARLES SCATCHARD

'Frankly I cannot see any real future for women's professional golf in the British Isles. And though I think – and hope – that we shall find the American proettes coming again, and yet again, I do not think there is much prospect of a British women's PGA coming into being.'

So I wrote in a newspaper article thirty years ago, when a team of US women professionals under the managership of Fred Corcoran – one-time American PGA Tournament Director and manager of the legendary Walter Hagen – made a 'missionary' tour of the British Isles.

It was a highly successful tour, but the opinion voiced at the end of it was probably then the opinion of the vast majority of British golfers.

Well, I should have known better. Not only is a British WPGA now firmly established, with some £250,000 of prize money at stake annually in a circuit extending over six months, but there is now also talk of a biennial 'Ryder Cup' match between the proettes of Europe and the US.

The British tour, of course, started only in 1979, and just as Fred Corcoran played such a big part in developing the American tour during the 1940s, so the present European proettes owe much to the vision and energy of their Tournament Director, Barry Edwards, and his wife, Carole.

Before the present British tour started, the former Curtis Cup player, Vivien Saunders, battled on virtually alone in the women's pro. ranks. But it may surprise a lot of present-day golfers to hear that there was a woman professional in Yorkshire half a century ago. She was Poppy Wingate, who acted as assistant to her brother, Temple Newsam professional Syd, and who in fact made one or two appearances alongside the men professionals in the old *Yorkshire Evening News* tournament before World War II.

Even so, the arrival of the US proettes in 1951 was very much a novelty. In a hectic two-week tour, during which they played eighteen competitive rounds in ten days, the Americans defeated a team of leading British women at Sunningdale, of top men amateurs at Wentworth, and took part with six leading men professionals in a then highly lucrative £1000 international foursome tournament at Ganton. It was a programme of continuous golf, travel and social events, which would have reduced many members of the so-called tougher sex to a state of exhaustion. But the American women carried it through with an abundance of charm, good humour and showmanship.

Four of six Americans who made the trip, among them 'Babe' Zaharias and Patty Berg, had in their amateur days played against British teams in Curtis Cup matches, and Mrs Zaharias had carried off the British women's title at Gullane in 1947. An Olympic champion javelin thrower, and a great all-round athlete, the 'Babe' pulled in the crowds with her reputation as one of the longest hitters of the ball women's golf had ever known.

It was, however, little freckle-faced Patty Berg from Minnesota who was the big favourite with the Ganton galleries. With feet so badly blistered that she had to soak them in methylated spirits between each round, she proved herself to be the most complete shot-maker in the side, and an irrepressible character to boot. Wearing an outsize man's type cap, Miss Berg won the first women's prize at Ganton, and the crowds warmed to her cheery and friendly personality. They rocked with laughter too as each of her male partners – Dai Rees, Fred Daly, John Panton, Arthur Lees, Charlie Ward and Bill Branch – blushingly received a resounding kiss at the end of each match.

One of the always-optimistic Mr Corcoran's freely stated ambitions was the eventual establishment of a British Women's Open Championship, run by the LGU, in which amateurs and professionals from all over the world could take part. Sadly Mr Corcoran did not live to see his hopes realized. But how far-sighted he was – and how short-sighted was I!

What it takes to become champion

DAVID DAVIES *Birmingham Post*

Nine rounds of match-play in all. That is what you have to survive and win to take the Amateur Championship. It is probably more perilous than any other golf championship, and for the amateur the pressures are manifest. Win, and your name goes on a trophy that already bears the names of Bobby Jones, Harold Hilton and

Michael Bonallack. Win, and you receive invitations to play in the
US Masters, the Open Championship, the World Series. Win, and
you get into the British teams for years afterwards. Lose, even as a
finalist, and you may never be heard of again.

But the winning is difficult. To do it you have to beat eight
opponents – men who may be good players playing well,
indifferent players having their day of days, players with
something to prove. At the same time you have to survive your
own inevitable day of weakness and you need, perhaps above all, a
dash of luck.

There will be, sometime in the week, a moment when your
match is out of your control, with nothing you can do to influence
it; and if your opponent does what he has to do, you are out.
Survive all these combinations, play well, hole your putts and hold
your nerve, and you may become Amateur Champion.

Let me take you part of the way through an Amateur
Championship. The place is Ganton, near Scarborough, in
Yorkshire, 1977. The player, Peter McEvoy. All that McEvoy
wanted, or at least dared to think about, before the Championship
started, was getting to the last eight. If he did, he felt, he had a good
chance of making the Walker Cup team.

But the draw had been unkind. His very first match was against a
man he had respected for years, fellow Midlander and Walker Cup
golfer, Geoff Marks, a man capable of beating anyone on his day.
McEvoy worked hard on his game, got to Ganton and found
Marks had scratched. Breathe again! That day more was to go right
for McEvoy. The holder, Dick Siderowf, drawn in McEvoy's
quarter, was beaten by the forty-seven-year-old Yorkshireman
Bernard Meldrum.

In the second round four more seeds, including such luminaries
as the American Amateur Champion, Bill Sander, and a former
holder of that title, Fred Ridley, also went out. Sander, illustrating
how anyone can beat anyone else over eighteen holes, lost to a
Scot, George Ellis, who confessed candidly that he had trained for
the match on 'beer and red wine'. Things, so far, were definitely
going McEvoy's way.

In the second round McEvoy met an unknown quantity, an

American, Robert F. Morman, who turned out to be a good player playing well. Morman had four birdies and an eagle against McEvoy, who had neither birdies nor bogeys and kept his head to win on the last green. It was the kind of unsung narrow squeak that most champions have to survive and McEvoy was to say later that Morman was the best player he had met during that week.

Thomas W. Barwick, another American, was next and he began by enquiring of McEvoy how long it would take for him to get to Edinburgh after the match. McEvoy was neither lulled nor fooled, applied himself and won six and five.

So far he was hitting the ball well, driving superbly and holing out confidently. But abruptly, in the fifth round, it all left him. He had to play Les Walker, a stocky, stubborn Yorkshireman and a fierce competitor. McEvoy was awful. He arrived on the sixteenth tee three down, at which point a Yorkshire supporter said to Walker, 'That's dormie then, Les.'

Walker replied, prophetically, 'You're never dormie when you can lose.'

Walker duly lost the sixteenth and seventeenth holes to pars, but when McEvoy bunkered his second at the eighteenth the way seemed clear to a Yorkshire win, despite the fact that Walker also bunkered his approach. When the two players arrived at their respective golf balls, a Walker win suddenly seemed a formality. His was a straightforward bunker shot, which he duly played well to eight feet. McEvoy, however, was in a horrendous spot, on the back downslope of the bunker on the right, plugged and barely playable. The pin was on the right of the green, leaving McEvoy nothing to work with; and he now had to try to extricate himself from a spot that would have had Gary Player shaking his head sadly and would leave most professionals wondering about taking a penalty drop.

But McEvoy, as he climbed into the sand, simply muttered: 'I can cope.' He did, with a shot that changed his entire career. He not only got the ball out, but placed it within ten feet of the pin. Around the green there was an incredulous silence followed by unbelieving laughter. The shot was not possible, but it had been played. Then, just to emphasize the point, McEvoy holed the ten-footer. Walker had absolutely no chance now with his putt, and two extra holes later McEvoy had won.

He had, in a sense, also won the Championship. In those moments the destination of the 1977 Amateur was all but decided. McEvoy went on to beat John Glover, to hold off one period of inspired play from Paul McKeller in the semi-finals, and to survive some of his own indifferent play in the final against Hugh Campbell.

It had been a classic Championship. Its winner, as he was to prove by retaining the title at Royal Troon the next year, was equipped to handle good luck and bad, to play well and win and to play badly and win. He had the character that every Amateur Champion must possess, which enabled him to say, in the face of the impossible, 'I can cope.'

A Scottish tragedy

GEOFFREY COUSINS

Golf spectators are so accustomed to looking at the stars from behind ropes that only the elders among them can recall the days when fairways were common ground for both watchers and players; when competitors often could not follow the flight of their drives for the horde of fans dashing to secure vantage points for the next strokes; when control was exercised, often with difficulty, by stewards using mobile ropes and bamboo staves; and when 'Players please' and 'Don't run' were oft-used exhortations.

At one time golf-watching was 'free-for-all' in a very real sense, because as late as 1925 no charge was made for admission to the course for the Open Championship. Gate money was imposed by the Royal and Ancient Club for the first time in 1926 – a modest half-a-crown (12½p) – and this innovation was forced by a tragic reversal of fortunes at Prestwick in the previous year, when a golfer lost because too many people wanted him to win. For although the records show that Cornish-born Jim Barnes won the 1925 Open Championship, the story of the day was the sensational collapse of Scottish-born Macdonald Smith.

Those two naturalized Americans spear-headed the transatlantic assault in the absence of both the holder, Walter Hagen, and his greatest amateur rival, Bobby Jones. And MacSmith, as he was known, was the form horse, having finished third in 1923 and again in 1924.

West of Scotland golf spectators have always been the most enthusiastic, and in the days before roped fairways were often intolerant of efforts to keep them in order. It was told of a previous Prestwick Open – Harry Vardon's in 1914 – that some miners entirely ignored the despairing cry of a steward 'Players please'. 'To hell with the players,' said one burly miner, 'we want to watch the golf!'

Given the traditional enthusiasm and the fact that 'MacSmith' was favourite, the stage was set for the tragic sequel. The former Carnoustie man made an unimpressive start with a first round of seventy-six against a record of seventy by Barnes, but in the next round he set up a new record of sixty-nine to take a two-stroke lead. Then Fate took a hand with the draw for the final thirty-six holes.

Nowadays the leading contenders for the last two rounds know they will be last or nearly last in the starting order, but in 1925 all the names of qualifiers went into the hat and the luck of the draw was to have disastrous consequences for Smith. His name emerged nearly last, whereas Barnes had an 8 a.m. starting time. The Cornishman did not take advantage of this opportunity to set the pace, for he took seventy-nine on his third round. Smith, round in seventy-six, increased his lead to five strokes with eighteen holes to go.

By that time Barnes was well on his way in the final round and so escaped most of the trouble which was to beset the leader. Long before MacSmith resumed play the large crowds of the morning had been swollen to record numbers as trains from Glasgow, Ayr, Irvine and Troon disgorged Scots – men, women and children – who swarmed on to the congested links prepared to enjoy themselves and cheer a Scottish victory. And in that atmosphere of elation and euphoria their hopes withered and died.

There was no hint of impending disaster as Smith began his last round and he negotiated the opening holes without mishap. Then, at the third hole, the Cardinal, where crowd control was notoriously difficult, there was a long hold-up while stewards tried to marshal the excited spectators. Upset by the delay, the mercurial Scot made a disastrous drive and the hole cost him six. At that stage it was a cloud perhaps 'no bigger than a man's hand', but it presaged the tempest which was to follow. Smith went from trouble-spot to trouble-spot, taking forty-two to the turn, where he faced the almost impossible task of coming home in thirty-six to tie with Barnes, who had by then finished his day with a round of seventy-four for a total of 301. At the short eleventh, hustled by the ungovernable crowd, which he knew would engulf him as soon as the ball was struck, he hit a wild tee shot which fell among the running spectators and rebounded into trouble. The hole cost him five, and that was the end. He struggled on to finish in eighty-two and lost not only to Barnes but also to two British players, Ted Ray and Archie Compston.

That débâcle was the direct result of a large unruly crowd invading a links which was unsuited to the accommodation and control of big galleries. It led to the imposition of gate money, which helped to ease the problem. But Prestwick, where it all began in 1860, had lost its place on the Open Championship rota.

What the gods decreed

PAT WARD-THOMAS *Country Life*

Looking out over the links shining in the evening light, at peace once more after the 1978 Open was done, I could not help wondering whether the Old Course had ever known a famous occasion come to a more fitting climax than the victory of Jack Nicklaus.

No other American golfer, not even Jones, Hagen, Sarazen or Palmer, has ever had as prolonged an influence on the championship, nor one more beneficial. He had competed for seventeen successive years and his presence, following that of Palmer in the sixties, had ensured that many other Americans would come and that the old championship would once again be the foremost golfing event in the world.

Not since James Braid in 1910 had any golfer been Open Champion twice on the Old Course. Nicklaus's victory meant that he had won all four major championships three times and more, a peerless tally that may not be approached for generations. It was therefore entirely fitting that he should reach this lonely peak at St Andrews. Everything there – the weather, the record crowds, the beautiful condition of the links, the ageless setting and the admirable presentation – ensured that the days would remain in our memories. We remember Nicklaus's victory in 1970 as well; but this Open was not scarred by tragedy such as the one which befell Sanders then.

It was a strange repetition of history for Nicklaus who, before both occasions, had had three years without victory in any of the great championships. There were those who feared that his powers, not of technique but of the abstract qualities with which he has been so remarkably endowed, were beginning to wane. Such doubts are now dispelled. Rarely have I seen him strike his shots with such precision or consistently balanced rhythm. Clearly he was in high confidence with all his clubs, but any number of possible putts in the first three rounds escaped him. Many thought that Watson, whose defence of his title was becoming increasingly impressive, would prevail.

That he did not was due in part, I think, to one of the capricious switches of the breeze with which the Old Course defends itself. When it turned from east to south-west on the last morning, Nicklaus was delighted, knowing that his greater experience of it might give him an advantage. Thus it proved. After seven holes Watson, whose putting had been uncertain, had dropped four strokes and was out of the running. Nicklaus then went ahead, but only marginally. His companion, Simon Owen, an engaging New

Zealand golfer, aided by confident striking and fine long putting, stayed within the stroke, as for a long time did Peter Oosterhuis.

The Old clearly was the course where Oosterhuis might regain something of the confidence he had lacked in recent weeks. He almost made the most of it, but as the plot gathered momentum and the leaders approached the closing holes, his putting failed him, an uncommon fault. Nonetheless, he and Nick Faldo, who finished only a stroke behind him in seventh place, had served the British cause splendidly. Faldo continues to progress in extra-ordinary fashion. His highest score was seventy-two and he has only been playing the game for seven years. The amateurs, fittingly headed by Peter McEvoy, had their finest showing in a long time, with four of them still involved on the long last day.

Meanwhile Raymond Floyd, who had practised with Nicklaus in the same wind the previous week, came from well-nigh nowhere with an extraordinary inward half of thirty-one, and posted a total which left those behind him precious little margin. Soon afterwards Tom Kite, who played so well in the 1971 Walker Cup match at St Andrews and who, with his fine simple style, has since developed into a consistent tournament professional, matched Floyd's total. So too did Ben Crenshaw, a likeable young man devoted to the game's history. He rejoined the fray with three birdies in the last four holes.

The moment of crisis was at hand for Nicklaus. Suddenly from being one ahead he was one behind. Owen, who made a splendid four at the Long Hole, chipped into the fifteenth hole for another birdie. Nicklaus's response was that of a rare champion. A perfect three at the sixteenth, and a careful four at the seventeenth, gave him command. Owen, unafraid to enter the fray, attacked just too much and Nicklaus had two strokes to spare. Throughout the round he had played hardly anything approaching a false stroke; and when destiny beckoned, his approach putting, always one of his greatest strengths, was true as true. When he walked on to the eighteenth green, the warmth of acclaim that greeted him was as much, I believe, for the man himself as for the supreme champion of our age.

Printer's error

DOUGLAS CAIRD

In 1945 I became owner and editor of *Fairway & Hazard*, a magazine devoted entirely to women's golf. My first issue dealt mainly with the forthcoming Curtis Cup Match which was due to be played under the captaincy of Mrs Baba Beck, the famous Irish international. Proudly I wrote a leading article which should have concluded with: 'And so, Mrs Beck, Good Luck and bring back to Britain that coveted Trophy.' Imagine my horror when I opened up the book. The last sentence of the article read: 'And sod Mrs Beck . . .' For that month, at any rate, *Fairway & Hazard* was a sell-out and graciously Mrs Beck, in return for six copies, forgave me.

PART TWO

Giants of the links

A vintage quartet

GEOFFREY COUSINS

Golf, like wine, has its exceptional years; and golfing students of astrology and heredity regard the period 1868-72 with special interest. For that lustrum saw not only the four successive Open Championship victories of young Tommy Morris, but also the advent of four boys who were destined to make significant contributions to golfing history. The first to arrive was Alexander (Sandy) Herd in 1868. James Braid, another Scot, saw the light in February 1870. Three months later Harry Vardon was born in Jersey, and in the following March John Henry Taylor made his appearance in North Devon.

Between them they won the Open seventeen times, and although Sandy was only once successful he was placed six times in the first three, and in 1926, aged fifty-eight, he won the match-play championship for the second time. In addition he twice beat Vardon in match-play finals in the late nineties when the Englishman was at the peak of his power. He also had the longest competitive career of the four, playing in the Open for the last time in 1939, at the age of seventy-one, and fifty-four years after his first essay.

I had the good fortune to see those great golfers, if not in their prime, at least when much of their old magic was still apparent. It was in 1921 that I had my first sight of Vardon in an exhibition match for the opening of the Hadley Wood course at Barnet. In the locker-room afterwards his partner, George Duncan, told me with characteristic emphasis and flattering over-estimation of the extent of my circulation: 'You can tell the world, young man, that Vardon has got back his putting.'

I was left with the impression that Vardon was vulnerable only if his putting broke down, but now incline to the view that his famed accuracy in the long game allowed him to treat with indifference the dictum of his great Scottish rival, Willie Park Junior, that 'the man who can putt is a match for anyone'. That might be true today, but eighty years ago wooden clubs were used extensively for second shots. Vardon and his contemporaries in their heyday had to play brassie, spoon or baffy (beautiful words now reduced to numbers) at ten or twelve holes in the round, so the emphasis was on the long shots to the green, a field in which Vardon was the acknowledged master.

In 1897, just after his first Open victory, he had a round of seventy-one at Newcastle, Co. Down, after going out in thirty-two, to finish the first round of a thirty-six hole final eleven up on J. H. Taylor. Taylor's anguished comment was 'He's not a man at all: he's a blooming steam-engine.'

I cannot give the lengths of the Newcastle holes at that time but it was, and still is, a championship links, and Vardon was hitting the gutta-percha ball with no more than seven or eight clubs. He normally carried two woods, four irons and a putter, and the most lofted club in the bag was equivalent to the modern seven-iron. Imagine the great variety of approach shots to be planned and executed with that modest armament. Try to estimate the skill and concentration required to recover from deep and unraked bunkers without benefit of sand wedge or even a niblick. Then look again at that seventy-one made more than eighty years ago and get some idea of true greatness.

Whereas Vardon was docile, non-partisan and equable in temperament, Taylor was fervent, pugnacious and tenacious, being both instigator and operator of new departures. As the principal founder of the PGA and a pioneer of public course golf in

England, he did much for the game. I remember seeing him in what should have been the forbidding atmosphere of a Whitehall Ministry when he argued the case for golf in Richmond Park with sceptical officials of H. M. Office of Works. He carried the day, and one of the proudest moments of his life was when he watched the Prince of Wales open the first of the two courses there.

In contrast to Taylor, who had no difficulty in expressing himself, often at length, with voice and pen, Braid had the gift of brevity with both instruments. He was sparing with words, not easily drawn into debate, but when, upon request, he did deliver an opinion, he answered often monosyllabically and always sensibly. In his shop at Walton Heath, now the caddies' shelter, most of the space was a work area where Willie Brown and Robert Horsbrugh, his principal clubmakers, plied their craft, and he had a desk in the corner at the back where he made out his meticulous accounts, wrote his prompt cheques, and was always ready to listen to any interrupter with a problem.

He was friendly to all, but particularly to those most in need of friendship. The very first time I saw him at Walton Heath, where I interviewed him on some matter, he put me completely at ease, answered my questions and then, lifting his lanky, bony frame from his chair, said: 'And now ye'll come along for some tea.' So for the first time, but not the last, I walked with him up the lane to his cottage, Earlsferry, to be regaled with tea and cakes by Mrs Braid.

Vardon, Braid, Taylor and Herd were the stars of the years before the Great War. They were all modest, hard-working men who played golf in the finest spirit and contributed much to its development and the status of the professional. It was a great privilege, as well as a pleasure, to know them.

One of the all-time greats

TOM SCOTT   *Golf Illustrated*

To most of today's golfers Harry Vardon is merely a name, yet this great man who created a record by winning the Open Championship six times, in 1896, 1898, 1899, 1903, 1911 and 1914, left his mark on golf in more ways than one. Apart from his record of six Championships, he was also the first player to use successfully the overlapping grip now used by golfers all over the world. The Vardon grip was one of the great steps forward in the game.

Harry Vardon was born in a little cottage close by the links of the golf course at Grouville in Jersey on 9 May, 1870, and he died at Totteridge on 20 March, 1937. Not long ago I made the pilgrimage to Grouville, to the Royal Jersey links, to see what remains of his birthplace and to capture in my mind's eye the sight of the slim, spindly-legged Vardon caddying for a few coppers to eke out the family budget.

It was for me a sentimental journey during which there came flooding back to me memories of the few times when as a lad I had seen him play. A quiet, slim man, dressed almost invariably in a tweed jacket and knickerbockers, Vardon was the epitome of golfing style. What always sticks in my mind was the complete ease with which he hit the ball. Unlike his great friends and rivals, the rangy, slightly ungainly Braid and the stocky, pugnacious Taylor, Vardon depended on the perfection of his timing rather than on power, and his record through the years proves that his method was a highly successful one.

In the way of successes Vardon just had the edge on the other two, but I could never succeed in getting the outspoken John Henry Taylor to agree that Vardon was better than he. 'Harry won a Championship more than I did,' was as far as 'J.H.' would go.

Then he would continue with a twinkle in his eyes; 'But he was a grand player.'

Taylor always told me that he was the first player to experiment with the 'Vardon grip', and I have no reason to doubt him; but it was Vardon who persevered and achieved success with it. When he started golf, like everyone else in those days, he used the two-handed grip, that is a grip where no fingers overlapped or interlocked; but having strong hands he started to think of a method of holding the club in a way which would give greater control. It is almost certain that Vardon, Taylor and Braid all talked about the grip and tried it out. Being close friends as well as rivals, this would be a perfectly natural thing for them to do: but it was Vardon who stuck to it and who made it popular.

There are some who maintain that Vardon was the greatest golfer of all time. But of course it is impossible to compare a golfer of one generation with another. Was Vardon greater than Jones or Hogan or Nicklaus? Who can tell?

What we do know is that before the arrival of Vardon, Braid and Taylor on the scene, golf had made comparatively slow progress as a game and none at all as a public spectacle, but the Great Triumvirate changed all that and their skill and rivalry stirred the country to such an extent that golf courses sprang up like mushrooms. Wherever they played crowds flocked to see them. They were the first heroes of the sporting public, the forerunners, albeit low-paid ones, of the great sports idols of today.

Before their time spectators at the popular golf challenge matches of the day were merely partisans who wanted the man from their home town to win. There were many quarrels and even fist fights at such matches. But Braid, Vardon and Taylor ended all that. Their skill and popularity drew enthusiasts who came not to see their local men win but simply to watch three great performers play golf.

An evergreen called Sam

BOB GREEN *Associated Press*

Edward VIII was King. Pius XI was Pope. Roosevelt was seeking a second term as President of the United States. Churchill was out of office and devoting his time to writing *Marlborough, His Life and Times*. Hitler occupied the Rhineland. In Cambridge, Massachusetts, John Kennedy was a student at Harvard. In the Philippines, Dwight Eisenhower was a Major. In Detroit, Michigan, a young boxer, one J. L. Barrow, who later became better known by his two first names, Joe Louis, was beginning to attract attention. In Atlanta, Georgia, an author named Mitchell was completing her first work, *Gone with the Wind*.

Africa had yet to emerge. We had not yet been promised peace in our time. The nightingale was still awaiting his cue to sing in Berkeley Square. The Great Depression gripped the western world. Sports offered escape from the grinding realities of economics. Jesse Owens won four gold medals in the Berlin Olympics. Glenn Cunningham held the world record for the mile at 4:06.8. Fred Perry took his third consecutive singles title at Wimbledon. Alf Padgham won the British Open golf title at Hoylake. And, at that time, in 1936, a loose-jointed young man came wandering out of the hills of West Virginia and won his first professional golf title in America. Fellow named Samuel Jackson Snead.

Almost half a century later, Sam is still with us, still competing, still capable of winning, still chasing the cherished dollar or pound, rand or yen, around the fairways of the world so vastly changed from that long-ago time when he won something called the Virginia Closed Professional Championship.

He has bridged the golfing eras. Nelson and Hogan, Cotton and Locke are his contemporaries. At the highest level of the game, in the US and British Opens, he competed against Hagen and Sarazen. And, at that same level, in the Masters, he has competed against Watson and Ballesteros.

'He's the most amazing athlete in the history of the world,' said Lee Trevino.

'His body is a God-given gift,' said Watson.

'Sam is unique, one of a kind, a natural phenomenon,' said Jack Nicklaus.

His record is incredible. He is credited with eighty-four official US PGA Tour titles, No. 1 on the all-time list. Nicklaus is second with sixty-eight. Snead is credited with 135 world-wide victories. He led the money-winning list three times, took the Vardon Trophy (for the low stroke average) four times, played in the American Ryder Cup team eight times (spanning eighteen years), won the World Seniors five times.

He won ten official titles in 1950. He won the 1946 British Open, three PGAs and three Masters, the last in a classic play-off against Hogan. Strangely, the title he wanted most, the US Open, always eluded him. He once made eight on the final hole to blow it. In 1979 he shot his age, 67, in the Quad Cities Open, a regular stop on the American Tour. The next day, competing against men young enough to be his grandsons, he bettered it, recording 66. With the growth of purses in the last two decades, he achieved his best money-winning year in 1974 at the age of sixty-two.

But the statistics, the records, don't begin to capture the flavour of the man whose career was, and is, coloured by twin trademarks: a brightly coloured straw hat and that pure, sweet swing which so successfully defied time.

The pure Snead, the essence of the character, was an odd mixture. He was, at times, naïve and gauche, the unlettered hillbilly. He was, at times, witty and charming. He could be profane and greedy. He could be mischievous and playful as a puppy. He has a delightful drawl and a still-twinkling eye.

He has achieved immortality. He is a member of various Halls of Fame, but that is not the test. True immortality is achieved when one's name is associated with classic locker-room stories.

Snead is linked, possibly apocryphally, with the best, the famous 'Gotcha' tale.

It seems Sam was practising for a tournament when a wealthy club member approached the great man and suggested a game. 'I'm busy, got no time,' said Sam. The member suggested they play for $1000 a hole. 'That,' said a delighted Snead, 'is the name of the game. What's your handicap?'

'No handicap,' replied the member. 'We'll play it head to head, but you have to give me two gotcha's.'

'Two gotchas?' queried a puzzled Snead.

'Two gotchas,' demanded the member.

Snead shrugged, agreed to the mysterious request and the game was on.

On the first green, Snead was away and had a putt for a birdie three. The member had hacked and skulled from rough to sand to trees and reached the putting surface in five. Snead crouched over the putt. As he began to take the club back, the member quietly approached from the rear, reached down, clutched Sam's privates and, at the top of his lungs, shouted, 'Gotcha!' The match eventually ended. Sam walked off a shaken man.

'How'd you do, Sam?' asked a fellow pro.

'Lost $17,000,' mumbled Sam.

'My God!' said the pro. 'How did that happen?'

'Did you ever,' asked Snead, 'play seventeen holes waiting for the second gotcha?'

Unfortunately, this story is not documented. Fully authenticated, however, is an exchange that took place in the late 1930s. Snead was playing in the Bing Crosby tournament on the West Coast, and had the first round lead. The next morning his business manager, a delightful pixie of a man named Fred Corcoran, telephoned from New York to congratulate Snead and informed him that his picture was that day in the *New York Times*. 'It's a fake,' avowed Snead. 'I've never been to New York in my life.'

And there was the time, in 1946, when an unwitting Snead did little to improve Anglo-American relations. He was on the train from Edinburgh to St Andrews for the first post-war British Open.

He shared a compartment with a dour and crusty Scot. Near the end of the journey, Sam, accustomed to the neat, manicured courses of America, gazed over the rolling unkept dunes and moors and enquired – pleasantly as could be – of his companion: 'What's that? Looks like an old abandoned golf course.'

'That, sir,' replied the indignant Scot, 'is the Old Course of the Royal and Ancient Golf Club of St Andrews. It is not now, nor will ever be, abandoned.'

As a product of the Depression years, Snead had a great fondness for the dollar and a deep and abiding suspicion of banks. There was a prevalent rumour that he kept his cash in tomato soup tins buried in his front garden. A tournament was being played near his home. A couple of his fellow pros, deep and merrily in their cups, were discussing Snead late one night. The tomato-tin rumour crept into the conversation. Scotch-inspired, they deemed it only fitting and proper to investigate. Transportation and a spade were secured. They went singing into the night.

Sam was awakened by the barking of dogs. He peered from his window and, by moonlight, saw two staggering figures digging great gouges in his lawn. He went howling from the house, blasting at them with a poorly-aimed shotgun. The intruders weren't harmed and disappeared, bleary and hysterically-giggling into the night.

The incident was over, but the investigation was interrupted. The rumour was neither proved nor disproved. It remained a mystery. Did Snead, in fact, bury his money in tin cans that had previously contained tomato soup? Years later, Snead was asked about it.

'A damn lie,' he snorted. Then, with a twinkle in his eye, 'I never used *tomato* cans.'

Moments with Ben Hogan

PERCY HUGGINS *Golf Monthly*

The first time I saw Ben Hogan hit a golf ball was two or three days before the start of the 1951 Ryder Cup match at Pinehurst, North Carolina, over the famed No. 2 course at that resort. I had met him two years previously when he had been the non-playing captain of the US team in the 1949 match at Ganton. At that time, because of the serious injuries he had sustained in a road accident in early 1949, it was thought that he would never play golf again, let alone championship golf. How wrong everyone was. He came back to win the US Open (for the second time) in 1950, and then won it again in the summer of 1951.

The practice ground at Pinehurst was appropriately named 'Maniac's Hill'. I can't help contrasting the circumstances of Hogan's first Ryder Cup practice there with the 1981 Open Championship at Royal St George's, where there was a special large stand to accommodate some of the hundreds who watched practice play. Ben's audience at Pinehurst that morning was precisely two – a newspaperman from New York and myself!

We watched Ben hit about a hundred shots. What impressed me was the way in which he took divots. They were long and shallow and began only about three inches in front of where the ball had been – vivid evidence of the way in which he made impact with his iron clubs.

While the caddy was collecting the practice balls we chatted. A remark was made about the irons he was using. He commented: 'I've had them for about ten years. They're worth their weight in gold to me. I wouldn't part with them for anything.'

With a twinkle in his eye, my American colleague said, 'But Ben, there's been a new Hogan model out nearly every year.'

35

Ben's eyes sparkled. 'Yes, I've tried them all,' he said, 'but I still use these.'

In the match itself, in the singles Hogan was two up with nine to play (over thirty-six holes) on Charles Ward, who was making a brave fight. At the tenth, an ultra-long par five, Hogan, for once, was off-line from the tee, amid trees. Ward was straight down the middle, but with no hope of getting home in two. For a moment it seemed as though Ward might narrow the margin to one, because Hogan could gain only a short distance from the trees, and was still far from the green. It was not to be. Hogan took his driver, hit the ball an enormous distance from the fairway to the front edge of the green, then holed a lengthy putt for the winning birdie four. Three up instead of only one up.

Two years later Ben responded to the needling, by some, that he could not be ranked as a truly great golfer until he travelled to Britain and won there. He entered for the Open Championship at Carnoustie. In those days, when everyone had to play in the qualifying rounds on the Monday and Tuesday, most competitors turned up only on the preceding Friday or Saturday. Hogan came a full fortnight before the event. It was the week of the British Women's Championship, which I was supposed to attend, but I persuaded my then sports editor that Hogan's first practice play in Britain was more important than the championship, as a story. He agreed.

Another Scottish golf correspondent and I watched Hogan for three days. It was a fascinating experience. On the practice ground the caddy did not have to move to gather the balls as Hogan rifled shot after shot to finish at his (the caddy's) feet. In practice rounds Hogan seemed to consider any shot to the green that finished more than twelve feet from the cup a poor one. On his third practice round he hit a fine drive at the par five sixth hole. When he got to the ball Hogan turned to his caddy – the opportunist Cecil Timms who had been on the spot to offer his services – and said, 'I want you to go up to the green. I'm going to hit three shots with a two-iron, one to land on the front left of the green, one on the front centre, and one on the front right. I want you to be able to tell me what each ball does after it pitches.' Timms went to the green. Hogan then hit the three shots exactly as he had said. Was there any doubt that he was going to win?

Only the greatest

JOHN MORGAN   *Daily Star*

The question is ridiculous and unanswerable – Who was the greatest of them all? Jack Nicklaus, you say, because of what he has won and the manner in which he does it. Byron Nelson, others claim, was better. Didn't he win eleven (or was it thirteen?) tournaments in a row? Dare you leave out Gary Player, winner of Opens on every continent that stages the game?

With some reluctance I dismiss them all in favour of that tenacious Texan, Ben Hogan. I shed tears over the film *Follow the Sun* in which Glenn Ford portrayed the great man. I shed tears for him again at Houston, Texas, in 1967 when, as non-playing captain of the US Ryder Team he astonished us all by 'dropping' Arnold Palmer for one of the series of matches.

When I had my first real interview with him at the US Masters in 1973 he still would not admit that it had been a disciplinary gesture, reprisal because Arnie had 'buzzed' the Champions golf course in his private plane. 'A captain never has to explain,' was all I could get out of him on that topic.

But about Britain and our Open he said plenty. Losing the 1955 US Open to Jack Fleck in a play-off was, he confessed, the biggest disappointment of his illustrious career. 'But my biggest thrill, without any question, was going over to Carnoustie in 1953 and winning your Open at the first attempt. I had never played in Britain and when I got to Carnoustie I began to wonder if they had called me over to get me beat. Conditions were appalling. I played in wind, rain and such freezing cold I began to wonder,

"What the hell am I doing here?"

'I wore two pairs of pants, a long cashmere shirt, two sweaters and a rainsuit which I put on and took off so often I wore it out!'

Hogan shot a first round seventy-three. Then seventy-one, seventy and sixty-eight for a 282 total which any of today's world stars would gladly accept for Carnoustie's next Open with only the slightest risk that the winner's cheque wouldn't go with it. Ben reckons he didn't play particularly well. 'What made it satisfying was the fact I had beaten conditions I had never known before.'

Ben was – and still is – far from extrovert: even these words had to be chiselled out of him. His absolute concentration on the job in hand is exemplified in this tale: he was playing in a tournament, stood on the tee at a par three and knocked his ball twenty feet past the pin. His playing partner holed in one. Ben said not a word, lined up his putt and knocked it in for a two. Next day, same hole, same playing partner. Again Hogan had the honour and this time knocked his ball twelve feet past. Again his partner holed in one (honest!). The impassive Hogan eyed his putt for quite a long time before knocking it in then, as they walked to the next tee, Hogan turned to his partner and said: 'That's the third time in a row I've made two on that hole.'

I wouldn't say he was a particularly hard man – except on himself, of course – but it is recorded that Gary Player, sharing my esteem for the great man, telephoned him for advice about his swing. The conversation went like this:

Hogan: 'Whose clubs do you play?'

Player: 'Dunlop's, sir.'

Hogan: 'Then I suggest you ask Mr Dunlop.'

The Hogan I saw was, of course, older and greyer than the film version. And he was walking with that hesitant stride, a legacy of the near-fatal car crash in 1949 which would have finished a lesser man. Yet he came back to involve himself again in championships. He won his first US Masters in 1951. His 1953 winning total of 274 (70, 69, 66, 69) stood unequalled until Nicklaus lowered it by one twelve years later with rounds of 69, 71, 64 and 69. I saw Hogan play just once, at the Houston Ryder Cup in 1967. He was in a four ball and I ducked out of watching the British team's final practice for a glimpse of The Master. From tee to green he was as near automated perfection as any human being could hope to be. But he had the yips. It was agony watching him on the greens trying to force himself to take the putter away from the ball.

In the end I had to turn away and I blamed a fly in my eye for the moisture running down my cheeks.

Bobby Jones – the unforgettable

GEOFFREY COUSINS

None of the 1500 people who crowded into the Younger Hall at St Andrews in 1958 to see Robert Tyre Jones receive the Freedom of the City will ever forget the climax to that moving and impressive ceremony, when the great man, crippled for several years, drove in his electric buggy, with the Provost of St Andrews as passenger, down the centre of the hall between ranks of applauding spectators, and out into the streets of the town where he had scored three of his famous victories.

Like many others, I was moved by this sight, having in my mind's eye a picture of the man in the pride of his youth striding British fairways like a conqueror. I wondered, too, what was passing in Bobby Jones's mind as he listened to that applause. Did he hear echoes of the cheers of long ago? Did he recall the almost hysterical applause which greeted his wonderful performance in the 1927 Open Championship when, with his trusty hickory-shafted clubs, unmatched except by his superb judgement, he covered four rounds of the Old Course in 285 strokes – an improvement of six on the record-equalling aggregate he had achieved the previous year at Lytham? Did he remember the tussles he had in the early rounds of the 1930 Amateur Championship before winning the title and so starting the Grand

Slam with which he crowned his short but meteoric career? And did he, perhaps, take a wry, sidelong glance at the memory of a nineteen-year-old coming to grief in the 1921 Open?

He had crossed the Atlantic not without reputation, for he had already played with distinction in the US Open and been a finalist in the US Amateur. But British golf was strange to him, and St Andrews was scarcely the most suitable ground on which to begin his initiation. The Old Course, fairly benign on the first day while he was compiling a thirty-six hole total of 151, showed its teeth on the following day with a strong wind and blustery conditions. The young American took forty-six to the turn, collected a six at the tenth, and after failing to recover from Hill bunker at the eleventh, made his exit from the Championship by very deliberately tearing his score-card to pieces and casting them into the wind over the Eden.

What a picture for the TV cameras if they had been operating! But this was long before the days of 'live' pictures, and there are no video play-backs for posterity. So I count myself fortunate in having seen Bobby in all his subsequent successes in this country, as he won the Open three times, the Amateur once, and overwhelmed his opponents in two Walker Cup matches.

That 1921 experience was salutary for the still immature, but wonderfully talented prodigy. He vowed he would never pick up again, and never did until he retired altogether from big golf after completing his Grand Slam. Thirteen national championships he won in the space of eight years – five US Amateurs, four US Opens, one Amateur and three Opens – and although the arguments rage about whether Jack Nicklaus has a better record I stay unblushingly by the side of Jones, who throughout his winning period was pursuing a second career – winning honours at three Universities and qualifying in law. He was not quite a weekend golfer, but almost. So he was not in constant match practice, as most championship golfers are today, and that may have accounted for the fact that his early play in important events was sometimes tentative, and that he was often vulnerable in eighteen-hole matches. But once he was in full song one could only wonder at the brilliance of this superb golfing machine.

He could hit the ball a long way when necessary, but there was no hint of ferocity or aggression in his stroke. The preliminaries were simple. A straightforward address with scarcely a waggle, and then that smooth, almost lazy-looking, backswing, the equally smooth acceleration to impact with all the effort expending itself in the controlled follow-through. He had the ideal physical attributes – sturdy of build, with large hands, he used his limbs and body in perfect co-ordination. In addition, he was mentally well-equipped for a task demanding concentration and judgement, even though every important match was a severe strain on his emotions and nerves.

There is no doubt that the stresses he suffered in championship and international play forced him to the decision to retire at the age of twenty-eight. Yet during his triumphant career he gave so much to so many people that he was revered as the outstanding example of excellence in golf, much as Harry Vardon had been a generation earlier.

In thirty-six-hole matches he was virtually unbeatable, but he often had crises in the eighteen-hole 'sprint' matches that were played at that time in the early rounds of British championships. (In the United States even quarter-final and semi-final games were over two rounds of the course.) Jones's vulnerability over eighteen holes led to several narrow squeaks in the 1930 Amateur Championship, none narrower than against Cyril Tolley.

The match took place on the Scottish mid-week half-holiday, and the already large crowds of regular spectators were swelled by many hundreds coming for the day from Edinburgh, Dundee and other places. And as the fairways were not roped off, as they are today, the Old Course soon became a battleground as hordes of spectators, not all of whom were disciplined, streamed along the narrow playing area intent only on seeing as much as they could of the 'match of the day'.

Since nothing else attracted the crowd's attention, the unfortunate homeward-bound players without galleries were engulfed by the approaching army and perforce had to suspend play until the tide had passed. Jones and Tolley were scarcely better off because, once they had driven, the fairway in front became black with running spectators and after the approach shots had been played they had to force a way through the crowds already encircling the green.

The match pursued a ding-dong course with first one player and then the other taking the lead, and they were all square going to the seventeenth, the famous Road Hole, where Jones had to hole from eight feet to snatch a half after Tolley had played a magnificent pitch over the bunker to lie dead for a four. Tolley had a ten-footer for the match at the eighteenth but missed it, and so they went once more down the first fairway. Tolley pulled his approach and his chip left him with a putt of about seven feet. Jones, on in two, had a four-yard putt which stopped inches from the hole, right on Tolley's line. It was an impossible stymie, and without it Jones would never have achieved the Grand Slam. He beat Roger Wethered seven and six in the final: won the Open at Hoylake, and back in the United States won both Amateur and Open titles to complete an astonishing quartet.

The crowd in the Younger Hall sang 'Will ye no' come back again?' as the buggy went down the aisle. But he never did come back, although he lives in many hearts, remembered not only for his superlative golf but also for his unassuming character, his warm-heartedness to all and sundry, and his unfailing sportsmanship.

A man for immortality

BOB FERRIER

'Golf is deceptively simple, and endlessly complicated. A child can play it well, and a grown man can never master it. Any single round of it is full of unexpected triumphs and seemingly perfect shots that end in disaster. It is almost a science, yet it is a puzzle without an answer. It is gratifying and tantalizing, precise and unpredictable; it requires complete concentration and total relaxation. It satisfies the soul and frustrates the intellect. It is at the same time rewarding and maddening – and it is without doubt the greatest game mankind has ever invented.'

Not bad, that . . . Perhaps the only way you could improve it would be to substitute for the word 'golf' the name of the author – Arnold Palmer. Palmer is essentially – he would not agree – a simple man, and there was a time in his career when he had so captivated America that it was 'Palmer for Governor', 'Palmer for Senator', 'Palmer for President'.

I have no particular right to write about him, since I am just one of the thousands of people who have crossed his path and shaken his big hand occasionally, in his marvellously full life. But I have been lucky with Palmer. I've seen what I believe to have been his greatest triumphs, and also what I believe to have been his greatest disasters – seen him rewarded, seen him maddened, by this perplexing game.

There is little doubt in my mind that his two greatest achievements were the Open of Troon in 1962 and the US Masters of 1964.

In 1962, Troon was burnt dry, with fairways of about the consistency of the Prestwick Airport runways. The ball bounced anywhere, everywhere. I remember sitting with him the evening before the championship began, in his room at the Marine Hotel, overlooking the course. He told me about his final practice round that day.

'At the fifteenth hole,' he said, 'I hit the very best drive of my life, as hard as I could, right in the middle of the clubface, exactly on the line I had planned down the middle of the fairway. When I got to the ball, it was four yards in the right rough, on a steep downslope, in a tangle of heather, the perfect shot that ends in disaster. Right then I decided to quit, and go home. I thought the course was just unplayable. But when I finished the round, still steamed up, I thought, "Well, the hell with it – it'll be the same for everyone. So I'm still here".'

He then went out and won the championship with a record score, and by a record margin.

And at Augusta in the 1964 Masters, he seemed to pour every

drive down the fairways into position A, smothered the flagsticks with a dazzling exhibition of approach iron play, and dominated the tournament from beginning to end, for a peerless victory. But there were other days.

Fifty years after the young Francis Ouimet had tied with the great English giants Vardon and Ray at the Country Club, Brookline, Massachusetts, and beaten them in the subsequent play-off, the 1963 US Open Championship was properly and evocatively returned to the same venue – and lo! there was another three-way tie. It involved Julius Boros, Jackie Cupit, and Arnold Palmer. For some reason that I forget, I was to have dinner with the Palmers that night, and when I reached their Boston hotel room Arnold was coming out of the shower, a towel clutched round his middle. He looked as strong as a fighting bull, ready that night to go in against anyone for the middleweight championship of the world. He was like a caged lion. He couldn't wait for the morrow. It was clear that neither Boros nor Cupit could possibly beat him in the play-off – he was going to mangle them both.

So in the restaurant, he plunged through the card – a big plate of cherrystone clams, an enormous slice of beef, baked potatoes, salad, apple pie and ice-cream, coffee, everything within reach. Alas, something went bump in the night – a cherrystone clam, I dare say – and to put it mildly, our man had a sleepless night with stomach trouble. At tee-off time next day, he was as weak as a kitten, and in fact on the tee said to Joe Dey of the US Golf Association, 'Joe, don't be surprised if you see me take off into the woods today.'

In the event, it was no contest. Arnold was beaten by both men – in any other circumstances no man would call them his peers. Even so, he remained in character. I have a vivid recollection of him on one hole, with the match beyond his grasp and having driven into the woods, finding his ball on top of a tree stump, two feet off the ground, 150 yards from the hole. Arnold flailed away at it without a second thought. He always did believe that if you can hit it, you can hole it.

In the US Open of 1966, at the Olympic Club in San Francisco, I left Winnie Palmer after nine holes of the last round, with Arnold six strokes clear of the field. Winnie said, 'Come over to the house and have a drink tonight.'

I said, 'Fine, thank you very much.'

Then she turned and said, 'Come over – win or lose.' It seemed a shade spooky. Arnold promptly squandered the six strokes to Casper, and next day, the play-off.

The next year, at Baltusrol, Palmer and Nicklaus went into the last day tied at level par, the rest nowhere. On the final round they matched strokes until around the fourth hole, when Arnold hit a lovely long iron from the fairway, some twelve feet below the hole. Jack followed him with a lovely long iron from the fairway, eight feet from the hole, a killer. Jack made the putt, Arnold did not.

On the next tee, Palmer 'bust a gut', as they say, going for the big drive, missed the fairway to the right, came up behind a tree, dropped another stroke, and it was good-bye championship. Not quite a disaster, that one – Nicklaus scored 65 against Palmer's 69 on that last round.

But there are not many grey areas with Arnold. There is a plaque let into the deep rough on one hole at Birkdale where he hit a monumental six-iron to the green in the Open of 1961. There is also a plaque on a tee at the Rancho Municipal course in Los Angeles where the man hit four successive tee shots solidly out of bounds.

Once after we had done some filming in Palm Springs, Arnold was planning to fly his own plane to San Francisco, en route to the Bing Crosby tournament. I was booked directly back to London from Los Angeles. But the Los Angeles airport was closed by fog, and I discovered that I could get a direct flight from San Francisco. So I made a rather tentative call to Arnold, explaining what had happened, and saying, 'Perhaps . . . maybe . . . do you think . . . would there be any space in your . . .'

He cut in, 'You wanna ride?'

I said, 'Well, yes.'

'You got it,' he said.

Having done some flying when aeroplanes had propellers, I sat close behind Arnold and his co-pilot, Darrell Brown, in the executive jet. I was able to identify all the flight instruments, radio and navigational instruments, save one. It was at the extreme end of the panel, calibrated 1 to 24, with two pointers all awry, and it beat me. Eventually I had to ask what that one at the end was. Arnold turned, gave me a very long look of the kind he used to reserve for the missed putt, and said slowly, 'It's a clock.'

If all this is rather subjective and over-personalized, you may say that I am a fan. This is not only because Palmer is the most exciting player I have ever seen, nor because of his achievement, nor because of the vast reward it has brought him. It is in part because he is an American who knows that the world does not end at the Statue of Liberty or the Golden Gate. It is because he has been the most international of American golfers since Walter Hagen. And I think it is in essence because Palmer, not always the world's best loser, nevertheless knows that the game is not about money. He knows, as few men before him, that the game is about pride, the game is about glory, the game is about immortality.

How Jack Nicklaus prepares for the Masters

KEN BOWDEN   *Golf Digest*

Every year the week before the Masters Jack Nicklaus spends three or four days at the Augusta National Golf Club. Nicklaus has now competed in twenty-three Masters, which means that, with this previous-week practice and pre-tournament rounds, he's played the course some 200 times.

The famed Georgia course has changed marginally over those years, but not enough to necessitate lengthy relearning visits. The same is true of most of the US Open and PGA Championship courses that Nicklaus habitually visits the week before the major events start. What, then, are his reasons for these time-consuming expeditions?

On the surface, little in the Augusta regimen seems likely to make any great contribution to his physical game or a profound difference to his psyche.

Generally, Jack gets in on Wednesday the week ahead of the tournament in time for an afternoon round and leaves on Saturday after a morning game, playing eighteen or sometimes twenty-seven holes on each of the two full days he's there. If there are other pros around he'll play with them, or he'll play with friends who are members if they ask him, or he'll play by himself.

During these rounds he checks his old yardages and studies the course extremely carefully – both its condition and any design changes – and he bears down hard on all the shots as he does on every golf stroke he ever makes. But the mood is relaxed. Invariably there's a writer or two on hand and a few club members or tournament workers getting a close-up look at Nicklaus's play. Between shots the conversation flows freely and easily. Occasionally, the small gallery will have a lengthy wait until Jack hashes out some golfing or other question that has caught his interest, or he gets into one of the finer points of agronomy with a member of the green staff.

Before and after the rounds there is practice. Nicklaus's physical preparation for the Masters has actually begun back in early January, and long before going to Augusta he will have known exactly what he wants to be able to do with the ball during the tournament, what if anything he is now doing with it that differs from his goals, and exactly what to work on during this penultimate practice period to correct any disparity.

Before-the-round practice is therefore usually just confirmatory and warm-up, and the after-the-round session – usually the longer one – tends to be corrective, if such is needed, or largely given over to finesse shots if all is basically well with the fundamentals. The long game is generally practised about twice as much as the short game, although that ratio has changed on occasion.

Off the course is also a relaxed time. There are no business meetings, but Nicklaus has daily, and sometimes lengthy, phone conversations with associates. He has many friends among Augusta National's members, and he enjoys the opportunity to 'shoot the breeze' with them as much as they do with him.

Dinner is usually fairly late because of the post-round practice and clubhouse talk sessions, and is taken either with local friends at their homes or in one of the town's choice eateries, often with writer types, whom Nicklaus seems to enjoy for their offbeat humour and unconventional perspectives on life.

Because Nicklaus has the good sense and ability to leave golf at the course, there is very little shop talk at dinner. Because he has essentially a put-down sense of humour, and can take the needle as well as he can give it, there's usually a lot of ribbing and joking, the loudest laughs reserved for the finely-phrased insult. Bedtime, at a downtown hotel, is invariably relatively early – Nicklaus has never been one for night life. Breakfast also is early.

In short, it's all very easy-going and unpressured and enjoyable, and therein lies one of the more obvious reasons Nicklaus makes such trips. Although he allocates all the time he feels is necessary to the physical side of golf on a day-to-day basis throughout the season, both the sheer volume of his other activities and the intensity of effort he gives to them make it difficult for him to immerse himself fully in the game mentally or emotionally for more than a few hours at a time when at home. One senses that to do just that is a prime purpose of his early practice trips to the sites of the major tournaments – as the other worlds drain away, the golfing juices flow back in. By the end of the soaking-up period, golf is No. 1 again.

Corollary to this is the atmosphere at the finer golf clubs where the majors are normally played, and especially at Augusta National. The course and all the other artifacts promote and facilitate excellence, and the aura of the place inspires it. There is also the not-inconsiderable factor of privacy. Once he's driven up Magnolia Lane no one is going to interrupt Nicklaus, or stick him in the eye with a pencil or pour beer down his neck jostling for an autograph. This time at Augusta National is his alone, to use how and when he pleases. We all know from those get-away-from-it-all vacations how soothing and restorative such times can be.

Are these Nicklaus's only reasons for the pre-major trips: to fine-tune his game while re-immersing himself in golf in stimulating surroundings – a sort of busman's holiday? Perhaps, but I think not.

Jack hates surprises – even supposedly fun things like surprise parties or a surprise visitor in an otherwise planned day. The reason he hates the unanticipated is that he cannot stand not to be ready for whatever is going to happen to him. Whatever the activity, from catching fish to negotiating a business deal to making a speech to seeking another major victory, he doesn't feel happy if he isn't 100 per cent prepared. Thus it has become an integral part of his life to get ready, to do everything he can ahead of time to ensure that, when the moment comes, he is totally equipped and conditioned to perform whatever task is at hand to the maximum of his capabilities.

In short, preparation with him isn't so much a choice as a compulsion – a motivator and driver perhaps as powerful even as his burning ambition to win. It's my guess that these previous-week trips, having over the years acquired a symbolism of their own as the ultimate act of preparation, are what finally put this marvellous golfing mind both at rest and in gear.

And never more so than for the Masters, the first of the majors and the mood-setter for the rest of the year.

Reprinted courtesy of *Golf Digest* magazine from the April 1979 issue. Copyright © Golf Digest/Tennis, Inc., 1979.

PART THREE

The way they saw it

Talking a good game

PETER DOBEREINER   *The Observer*

Once upon a time before you and I were born it was the custom of
newspapers to carry reports of sporting events. Our correspondent
would go along to, say, a cricket match and describe what he saw.
'Grace dispatched the crimson orb to the confines for the full
complement.' And much, much more in similar captivating style.

These days readers are not interested in what a player did. They
are fascinated to learn what a player *said* he did. Unless a sportsman
can talk a good game he is nothing. I am old enough to remember
when a craze for quote-journalism first fired the imagination of
sports editors and, as a practitioner in the field, it was uphill work,
I can tell you.

At a tournament in Yorkshire Neil Coles and Bernard Hunt
were playing together. Of course, being professionals, they were
never favoured with the use of their Christian names, thereby
becoming the source of frequent nightmares for the late Henry
Longhurst, the pioneer TV commentator.

Coles and Hunt were professionals of the old school, brought up
in the tradition that sportsmen should be seen and not heard. They
simply could not take to this new-fangled idea of answering
questions; and in those early interviews they responded mostly
with embarrassed grunts. On this occasion they had both scored

well and were duly wheeled into the press tent to be grilled for the day's quota of quotes. Hunt first. 'Drive, six, two putts. Drive, wedge, two putts . . .' The recital continued to the fourteenth hole. 'Drive, four, two putts.' At this point Coles, who was just beginning to grasp the fundamentals of the new journalism, gave a faint cough and raised one eyebrow about a millimetre. Hunt stopped his recital and looked at Coles in bewilderment.

'Aren't you going to tell them about the fourteenth?' whispered Coles.

'The fourteenth?' said Hunt. 'Regulation par.'

'No,' hissed Coles, 'you know . . .' (Say what you like about us sports writers but we can sniff a story.)

'What happened at the fourteenth?' we bayed. It was like drawing teeth; but we persisted and bit by bit it came out. As he was addressing the ball for his approach shot Hunt's club was struck from his hands by lightning.

Eventually we had our story, justifying the new system – for it was almost as good as if we had seen the incident for ourselves. But try as we might we couldn't get much of a quote out of Hunt. 'What did you do when the lightning hit you?'

'I picked up the club and hit the ball. Front left, about twenty feet.' It was a start.

How times have changed. Ten years later the players had mastered the art of the quote. When Lee Trevino was hit by lightning at the Western Open he did thirty minutes of stand-up patter without drawing breath and he had a column of quotes in every newspaper. That is why he is a superstar.

These days young professionals are taught the art of the quote at the American qualifying school and they have to sign a declaration agreeing to co-operate with the media at all times, meaning that they must be ready with a quotable quote at the drop of a tape recorder.

The most important time for quotes is before a tournament when the newspapers are obsessively devoting columns and columns to reports of what is going to happen. This is one of my favourite journalistic exercises and I live for the day when I master the art of prognostication to such a degree that it will not be necessary to report the actual event at all. I shall simply write: 'The Open Championship was played yesterday and turned out exactly as I forecast five days ago. Back numbers are available from the circulation department.'

Arnold Palmer is the absolute master of the quote and I cherish particularly his reply to a quote-hungry writer before the US Open championship. 'Do you think the guys can shoot low on this course, Arnie?'

'Waaall, any time you drive the ball in the fairway, hit all the greens and make a bunch of putts then you have a chance to make a score.'

That is straightforward enough, but there are pitfalls in the golfing quote and it may be helpful if I offer a little advice on the art of interpretation.

Thus the sentence 'This is a magnificent test of golf' can be translated as 'I hold the course record.' Likewise, when Dave Hill is quoted as saying 'This course is nothing but a cow pasture' he is really saying 'I missed the cut.' Beware, too, of Gary Player's favourite quote: 'This is the finest golf course I have ever seen, of its kind.' That is verbal shorthand for 'The Commissioner has warned me that the next time I criticize a host club in public he will have my guts for garters.'

When professionals are talking about their own play their remarks can only be properly understood if you happen to know their scores. I have therefore invented a new form of punctuation which I hope will be universally adopted by newspapers for golfing quotes. Here is how it works.

Jerry Pate led the first round and said: 63 I really enjoyed playing this superb course which has been beautifully prepared for the championship 63. Or: Larry Nelson commented: 75 They could do with lowering the cutters of the fairway mowers: I had a lot of flyers 75. Or: Lanny Wadkins snarled: 82 I'd like to get hold of the clown who set those pin positions and give him a lobotomy – with my wedge 82.

By now we experienced hands, both players and writers, have refined the quotes business to a fine art. I glance at the scoreboard and notice that David Graham, for instance, has been posted with a score of 76. A few years ago this would have required a complicated ritual involving a tape recorder and laborious transcription, followed by the editing out of any fruity adjectives and then the writing of the rough draft. Now, under the mutual trust system, the process can be streamlined.

Self: How?

Graham: Tripled five.

I can now go straight to the typewriter and begin: 'David Graham's challenge faltered with a third round 76. An otherwise solid performance was marred by a torrid seven at the innocuous 370-yard fifth hole where the players enjoyed the help of a light following breeze. Graham reeled from the course ashen faced and groaned: 'I played that hole like an arthritic granny.'

You may purse your lips and mutter about a decline in journalistic ethics but it is necessary to invent quotes more and more these days because professional golfers are gradually losing the power of speech. Already adverbs have been eliminated entirely from their vocabulary. 'I hit the ball super but putted just horrible.'

Some of these semantic murderers have gone further and limit themselves to the use of one adjective only, employing it on every possible occasion and sometimes in the middle of a word, thus: 'I played a low com-xxxxxx-pression ball.'

These developments in the world of golf reporting have transformed our lives. We cannot waste time enjoying the sunshine and fresh air on the golf course because hard necessity requires us to produce quotes. For reasons which I have explained we mostly have to invent such quotes, putting a gigantic strain on the imagination. The only way this can be achieved successfully, day after day, is by the use of artificial stimulants. Greatly against my natural inclination, and indeed to my abhorrence, I myself have occasionally to resort to the use of hallucinatory drugs, of which alcohol is the only form available in golf clubs. So if you should happen to see a golf writer in the bar while a tournament is in progress, please suppress that unfortunately common instinct to remark sneeringly: 'I thought you reporter chappies were paid to watch the golf.'

We are sensitive to such ignorant jibes. Just remember that as we force ourselves to swallow that hateful amber fluid through clenched teeth we are actually performing a difficult and distasteful task *for your benefit* and in order to support our families.

Leonard Crawley – the man

DONALD STEEL   *Sunday Telegraph*

Even in a ten-gallon hat, Leonard Crawley was unmistakably British. At the US Masters Tournament in Augusta each spring, where he became almost as familiar as Arnold Palmer, he could never pass as one of the crowd. Heads turned, admiring eyes blinked and mouths opened. In an atmosphere of gay informality, his Walker Cup blazer and half-eye spectacles were far from normal apparel; and nobody was too familiar with the fiery colours of the I Zingari Cricket Club tie.

It took a while for the American writers to get used to Leonard. Not until the day at the 1957 Walker Cup match at Minikahda, when 'your correspondent' fell asleep at his typewriter, misjudging the effect of a combination of heat and a lunchtime bourbon or two, were the Americans quite sure whether he was a friend or foe.

The acquisition, in 1959, of his famous red suit and the first of his cowboy hats persuaded the average American newspaperman to picture him not as the severe military type, but as a most likeable fellow with a touch of the clown in his make-up. Very soon he was elected a member of the American Golf Writers' Association and, in 1968, at the US Open at Oak Hill, he was presented with a blow-up of a World War II portrait of himself in his RAF uniform.

Not the least of Leonard's charms was his ability to impersonate and to tell stories, but the respect and admiration which built up amongst those who knew him centred upon his supreme skill at games which made him one of the finest all-round sportsmen of the century.

Even at the age of sixty-six, he could tee-off with Gene Sarazen and look every inch a Master. The crowd would recognize the beautifully unhurried tempo as a matter for envy and realize they were watching a swing quite out of the ordinary. But in talking about the background of the man who, in 1932, scored Britain's only point in the Walker Cup match when he could, if he had wished, have been packing his bag to take part in the controversial bodyline cricket tour in Australia, it emerged that the Crawleys are one of the most remarkable of all sporting families.

'I was born into a family of games players and read stories of my great-grandfather playing cricket 135 years ago. He had three sons, all of whom played for Harrow, and the eldest, George Baden Crawley, as captain of the Harrow XI, was asked to play for the Gentlemen against the Players at Lords. But great-grandfather would not allow his son to accept this singular invitation. Grandfather in his turn had a large family, four of his sons playing for Harrow, three for the University and my own father, a sailor, for the Royal Navy.

'I was the eldest of the next generation of brothers or first cousins and we were encouraged to play all games as soon as we could stand, except golf, which was taboo. Uncle Cavan was the only member of the family who played golf, but he was regarded as a freak. This idea of golfers being freaks was quite common sixty years ago but I hoped to show that it was the best natural ball-game player who made the best golfer.'

Leonard had a notable career at Harrow, during which his sporting talents really began to flourish, and then three years at Cambridge, at the end of which, in 1925, he went to the West Indies with MCC.

'My first introduction to golf at Cambridge came when I was woken by my landlady, the faithful Mrs Warnes, and told that the University captain, Eustace Storey, had arrived to say that the Society were one short for a match. I spent a most enjoyable weekend as Bernard Darwin's partner, although I dare say I should not have taken things so easily if Eustace Storey had warned me that Bernard could be the most difficult of all foursomes partners.

'In my last year at Cambridge I won my Blue by beating Bobby Speed for the last place in a play-off and then lost my single in the University match to an American who drove with an iron.

'The seed had been sown, and although I had no intention of giving up my cricket, I was determined to get down to this game of golf. As a result of becoming a preparatory schoolmaster, I acquired the habit of hitting some golf balls every day and, a few years later, became the worst English champion until then. Rude things were written about my victory.

'Even ruder things were published when I was sent to America with the Walker Cup team the following summer, but I beat George Voigt and, returning to London after being headmaster of a school near Moffat which, alas, had to close, I decided to learn to play properly.

'I went to Henry Cotton for a weekend in Brussels and he gave me his whole time and charged me a hundred and twenty quid. But I have played on his method ever since. He taught me everything I know about the game.

'Cotton was always supposed by the pundits in golf to be no teacher. Well, I entirely disagree. If you had ability, he was the best teacher of anything I have ever attempted and I have attempted a good many amusing pastimes. He simply knew his subject from A to Z. I think he got a poor reputation because of his enormous charges and because he was not so interested in those without great ability.

'At the same time as this, I used to try and keep up my cricket. I used to play about once a fortnight for Essex and enjoyed it quite enormously. I had a method of training myself, which was to play in a very poor club match and make as many as ever I possibly could out in the middle, rather than in a net. I was twice hit on the nut in a net and I was always terrified.'

Did he ever find that golf and cricket conflicted?

'No, that is the most awful rubbish. There are dozens and dozens of great batsmen like the Fosters, Frank Mann, F.S. Jackson, Hutton, Hammond, Compton, Dexter, Cowdrey and Graveney who could all have been first class golfers if they had paid attention to it. I never forget what Ranji said of games: 'The head of the striking implement must be supported by the wrists and this applies to all games from cricket to golf.'

The modern generation is probably not aware what a mighty fine cricketer Leonard was. Altogether he made about twenty first-class hundreds. Small wonder that Guy Morgan, a Glamorgan and Cambridge medium pace bowler, once said that the only way to bowl at Leonard was to 'let it go from thirty yards and hide behind the umpire'.

The war years were responsible for golf acquiring an eminent, new critic. 'All my life I had wanted to write about games, as I thought I knew something about them, but I couldn't find an opening. There was the usual Fleet Street business about "What experience have you had?" to which the reply was: "very little". And then they always wanted to suggest that you should go and write for some local paper which would be absolutely guaranteed to knock any respectability out of your writing.

'I had given up in despair when suddenly I came across Robertson Glasgow, one of the greatest writers of his time, and an old cricketing friend, who put me in touch with the *News Chronicle*. A year later they offered me fifteen guineas a week as cricket correspondent, but, by an extraordinary coincidence, I heard from Lord Camrose by the same post that he wanted to see me with a view to appointing me to his sporting-room staff on the *Daily Telegraph*.

'He promised to employ me as soon as the war was over, but when I told him that I had been offered a job on the *News Chronicle* right away, he immediately appointed me as golf correspondent at twenty-five guineas a week, back-dating it to the first of January.'

Much has changed since Leonard set out in 1945 to write on golf with George Greenwood, his predecessor, as chaperon for one year. 'This is a very amusing thing because I have never felt any embarrassment about writing of the game as I saw it, but it led to two other writers spreading the rumour that George Greenwood was writing all my stuff and that I would never make the grade.

'Anyhow, all ended happily and, if I had had a chance of

changing my life at any time during the last twenty-five years, I certainly wouldn't have done so.'

Leonard continued to play for England and in championships. In fact Michael Bonallack and Rodney Foster are the only men who have played more times for England. It is true to say of him that good techniques interested him more than good scores and he often found it hard to understand how certain players with obvious flaws could manage to get round under 70. Perhaps because games always came so easily to him and he had always done things so correctly, this was understandable. His own swing was a model and I remember Bill Campbell, the great American amateur, saying 'You can't help playing well against Leonard,' instancing that Johnny Fischer in 1938 and Bud Ward in 1947 both played 'career rounds' against him in Walker Cup matches.

In his later years, Leonard liked nothing better than to help young players build up their games. I asked him to outline the basic principles of a good technique and to say a little about teaching, which first interested him in his days with Cotton.

'I've always thought that teaching has been bad in all games in this country and, because of that, we, as a race, are rather bad learners. As I see it, American teaching is far and away more thorough than ours; Americans will break down the basic principles of all games before they really get going and they work at them as we never have.

'The difference between golf now and when I was first playing is that our young people have begun to take basic principles very seriously and that is why there are so many good amateurs today. I have the immense pleasure of spending a lot of time in winter at Worlington with the Cambridge side, and I compare it sometimes to when I was in the Cambridge side and never ought to have been. Nobody in those days ever thought of having a lesson. We scarcely talked golf. But these Cambridge boys today have all read everything there is to read and, if you give them a hand and put them on the right lines, there is no doubt that they are very, very responsive.'

I asked what points he would emphasize to a new, young pupil.

'The first thing I would do is to see that he held the club

properly. Secondly he must be impressed by the importance of balance; you can't get balance without footwork and you can't get footwork unless you learn it without a ball.

'I have never forgotten Joyce Wethered's remark: "On the rare occasions when I am playing my best, I feel that nobody could push me off my right heel at the top of the swing and, at the other end, I feel nobody could push me off my left foot." That is the perfect description of what balance should be.

'After balance, I go with Bobby Locke on swinging the club rhythmically. I don't believe in "quick flick Dicks". My criticism of British professional golf is that too many are too fast. They have never been taught to hit the ball smoothly. I think rhythm comes from the ability to copy, or the old monkey instinct. I think I could copy a style I admired even if it meant picking one's nose with one's elbow half-way through the downswing.

'I have never met any player, amateur or professional, who hasn't benefited from going *slightly* slower *than that which seems natural to him*. The reason that I got a rather laborious swing, or developed one, was that my first hero was Cyril Tolley and my next was Bobby Jones. Both swung the club slowly and, whenever I have been out of form myself, I have always gone back to the practice ground and made myself go slower. Snead has said that when he wants to hit a long one, he takes the club back slower, winds himself up and then really canes it.'

Being in Leonard's company, as I was so often, was never dull, and I had more fun with him, and from him, then with anyone else. Of the more easily recountable tales, there was the occasion at lunch one day when a Japanese director of Honda, holding a voluminous brandy glass, was urged by Leonard to be careful not to fall in.

Once, at the French Open, he had to rescue his lower dentures from his bag of practice balls before lunching with the Duke of Windsor. At Calcutta Airport, when an engine fault forced an unscheduled night stop, he wrote a curt one-word reply across the forty-two questions an immigration official had invited him to answer.

I would like to end with a story he told about the role of the hands in golf. 'If I were to criticize Cotton's teaching at all, I think he over-stressed the importance of using hands, but he made a profound observation to me once. He was trying to teach L. G. Brown, the great footballer and eminent surgeon. Brown had made every effort to learn a good style but he couldn't make his hands work fast enough to get any length and asked Cotton why he couldn't hit the ball any further.

"Because," Cotton replied, "you haven't got speed of hand. That's something which makes the club-head wag faster at the right moment, but," he said, "you can't teach it, you can't learn it, and you can't sell it. If I could sell it, I would sit in a window in Piccadilly and be a millionaire in next to no time. You've either got it or you haven't, and that's that".'

Leonard died in 1981. That he 'had it' there is no doubt, but he had much more besides, and it was this extraordinary combination of talents and charm that we shall be pleased to remember.

More to life than golf

KEITH MACKIE

As a rule of thumb, sporting heroes are best kept at arm's length. It is a sad fact that the seemingly clean-cut champion who dominates his sporting arena often, when seen in close-up, displays his warts and his lack of life's finer qualities.

But I'd like to pay tribute to a golfer who was one of those rare characters that look even better in close-up than at long range. He was Tommy Armour – winner of the Open Championship, the American Open and PGA titles and one of the original twelve members of the American Hall of Fame.

Most professional golfers of the thirties and forties bemoaned the fact that they were born too early, that the vast rewards of modern golf were no more than a dream when they were at their peak. Certainly Byron Nelson, who won eleven American tournaments in a row, collected less for that unrepeatable feat than some modern players can command in appearance money for merely turning up on the first tee.

Tommy Armour did not have that problem. Having made his reputation during the days of Bobby Jones, Gene Sarazen and Walter Hagen, he invested his relatively modest income from a host of victories in golf equipment companies in which he became a major shareholder. His first book went straight to the top of the American best-sellers list, the first sports book ever to enter the charts. He rapidly established himself as the best-known teacher of the game in the world, and he topped off a well-rounded career as an incisive television commentator.

Born in Edinburgh in 1896, Armour took his golfing talent to America at an early age. He had the unique distinction of playing for Britain against America in 1921 as an amateur and then playing for America, as a professional, in the forerunner of the Ryder Cup in 1926. He had the good grace, in that match at Wentworth, to lose his singles match to Aubrey Boomer and also his foursome, in partnership with Joe Kirkwood, to Boomer and the redoubtable Archie Compston.

Despite his golfing achievements and his fabulously successful career, Armour refused to take himself seriously. He had a simple, home-spun philosophy which kept life and mere golfing attainments very clearly separated. When I talked to him in 1963 he expressed his feelings in typically terse and graphic terms. Sharp, intelligent eyes twinkling under bushy brows, he commented: 'It's nice to be a good golfer and win championships, but hell, being the finest golfer in the world never cured anyone of polio.'

Not surprisingly, a man who could look at his own life with such candour had few inhibitions when it came to discussing other topics. Having played top class golf on both sides of the Atlantic, he was well qualified to comment on the differences between them and us. 'British pros are fine players,' he said, 'but I've often wondered if they get enough encouragement. My philosophy in life is that a pat on the back will do a lot more than criticism.

'The only playing difference is in the ability from fifty yards. Everybody misses shots, but it's the American ability to turn fives into fours that is so important. They're good at the short game because they practise, practise, practise and their equipment is fantastic. Their wedges are like surgical instruments.'

Armour took a characteristically contrary view on the question of slow play. 'There seems to be a fashion in Britain that the golfer who catches the public eye is the one who smashes into the ball, cracks it on to the green, hits the ball at the hole, takes three putts, looks round and says: "Well, that was nonchalant enough!"

'If I go out and casually push it around in two-and-a-half hours for 73 and you go round in four-and-a-half hours and do a 66 – who is the better golfer? These tournament professionals have nothing else to do, you know, they've got nowhere to go in the afternoon. This can be a little agonizing for some people, but who said that golf should be played fast? The tempo of the game has slowed down as its efficiency has increased.'

Tommy Armour provided a clear refreshing voice in a sport which is often cluttered with unthinking verbiage. He graced the game as a player, teacher, author and commentator. 'I would rather be remembered for being a nice fella than for being a golfer,' he said four years before his death. The man who treated life as life – and golf as only a part of it – is remembered vividly as both.

A stroke of blarney

JACK MAGOWAN   *Belfast Telegraph*

Fred Daly chuckles like a naughty schoolboy when he talks about the biggest bluff in the history of hoodwink. For he was the one who pulled it off, in a tussle with Henry Cotton in the *News of the World* Match Play Championship of 1947.

Daly had won the Open Championship at Hoylake a couple of months before, but it was the cool, calculating Cotton those Royal Lytham crowds had come to see. Let Fred himself tell the story: 'I remember the game as if it were yesterday. It was a crackerjack affair, the first of many great battles I was to have against some of the world's top names in match-play.

'I had been two up on Henry leaving the fourteenth green. The fifteenth at Lytham in those days was a par-five hole spanning most of 460 yards. We both hit good drives, Henry just a fraction longer than me. With the wind blowing across the hole, the second shot was always a wood, but I decided to try a bluff. "Give me that battered old cleek," I told my caddy, loudly enough for all to hear, especially Henry; then proceeded to slam a big shot full bore under the wind and straight at the flag.

'It was one of the best shots I ever played in tournament golf. At the same time, I wasn't sure whether the ball was home or not, and neither was Henry. This much I was sure of, however; the maestro wouldn't stoop to hitting a wooden club after I had hit an iron. And if I couldn't make it home with an iron, then he couldn't.'

The Daly bluff worked. Cotton played a two-iron, pulled it wildly off line, and ended up conceding the hole to a perfect Daly birdie. The gallery was ecstatic. The happy-go-lucky little Ulsterman was now dormie and all set to prove once and for all that his Open victory was no flash in the pan.

The police escort arranged by Cotton for the afternoon final was still necessary, but for Daly! Fred was about to become the first golfer since James Braid to lift both Open and Match-play titles in the same year, an elusive double accomplished by Braid in 1911, the year Daly was born.

Naturally, the clubs Daly used in that history-making era are among his most treasured possessions, and they include that famous cleek, or '2-X iron', as Fred calls it – a shallow-faced club which only one player in a thousand can ever use. With it, the wiry, steel-wristed Portrush man could have knocked the cap off your head at 200 yards' range. Sam Snead wasn't exaggerating when he once called Fred 'a prince among long-iron players'.

An Open Championship triumph is the Everest of every golfer's ambition, yet Daly might have won the title twice, perhaps even three times. Not until Jack Nicklaus shot a 66 and 68 at St Andrews in 1964 for second place behind Tony Lema had there ever been a last-day surge quite to match Fred's 69, 66 finish at Troon in 1950;

or for that matter, his opening two rounds at Lytham two years later. It seemed that nothing could stop him, when he spreadeagled the field with scores of 67 and 69 that year for a five-stroke lead at the half-way stage. But something did – a gale-force wind – and he eventually took third place again, this time behind Bobby Locke.

Pat Ward-Thomas saw a lot of Daly in those days, and waxed eloquent about him in *Masters of Golf*. 'Fred at his best was the finest British competitor of his day next to Cotton. He was capable of playing unanswerable golf, especially in match-play. I can see him now, strolling along the fairways of Wentworth in the Ryder Cup match of '53 and putting an American called Kroll to the sword with golf of extraordinary brilliance. He was round in 66 before lunch (and six up) and long putt after long putt trembled on the lip of the cup. The previous day he had nursed Harry Bradshaw through a long and desperate foursome, and at the end holed from four yards for victory. For those two days Fred was a very great golfer. They were the summit of his career.'

And the key to Daly's attacking game? 'Confidence and a cool head are a golfer's best allies,' insists Fred, now in his seventies. 'I always went into a match feeling I could win. Even when Lloyd Mangrum hit me with everything but his driver at Ganton back in 1949, I still felt I could take him in the end. I didn't, but I felt I could!'

This was an extraordinary golf match, certainly one of the greatest in Ryder Cup history. In those days, Fred played a driver that was two inches longer and an ounce-and-a-half heavier than normal, and for five holes Mangrum kept kidding him about 'those sledge-hammers you use for clubs.'

'If I had sticks like those, I'd use them for fishing,' teased the American, who looked just about all-in as he went for lunch. He had holed the famous Scarborough course in 65 shots, yet was only one up.

The fireworks didn't end there. By the time the dust settled, Daly himself had collected twelve birdies in thirty-six holes, and lost! 'The greatest game I never won,' he recalls with a grin.

This lovable Irishman hasn't always played pressure golf, however. When a St Andrews University team visited Balmoral, in

Belfast, some years ago, Fred played in the match, but not as Fred Daly. Instead, he was introduced to the unsuspecting Scots as 'Willie Frew, our bar steward'.

Imagine the perplexed look on two young faces when 'Willie' took an iron off the first tee, hit it yards past everybody else, and then proceeded to play the first six holes of the day in three-under-fours. At last, one of the guests couldn't restrain himself any longer. 'If this guy is a steward here, I'm sure glad Fred Daly isn't playing today.'

Interviews with golfing history

LIZ KAHN

TONY JACKLIN after winning the 1969 Open Championship at Royal Lytham and St Anne's:

A. Jacklin	68, 70, 70, 72 – 280
R. J. Charles	66, 69, 75, 72 – 282
P. W. Thomson	71, 70, 70, 72 – 283
R. de Vicenzo	72, 73, 66, 72 – 283

'I just don't know what to say. At the beginning of the week I thought, if I can get a good first round I stand a chance of finishing well. I had a good first round, a good second round, and so it went.

'Today, I tried to forget it was the Open Championship. I tried to play each shot as it came. I tried not to panic, but I was never as nervous in my life as I have been these last two days.

'I didn't know what to do with myself. I was blaming everyone for putting me off too late, expecting everyone to start at six so that I could play at nine.

'Last night I was so jumpy. I watched golf on TV, saw myself, and it brought it all back so that I got as nervous as when I was playing. I felt, there's no way I am going to sleep if I go to bed – I'll look at the ceiling and plan tomorrow's round over and over again, so that I will have been round the course twenty-five times before I get to the first tee.

'I decided the only sensible thing to do was to take a sleeping pill. It's not dope, so don't go making a big thing out of it. I took the sleeping pill at eleven-thirty and this movie on TV finished at twelve-thirty. I don't remember the end. Bert (Yancy) said I was holding a cigarette in my hand and my eyes were dropping. So he put out the cigarette, helped me upstairs, undressed me and slid me into bed next to my wife who was already asleep. I slept for eight hours and it was wonderful.

'I feel wonderful about winning. It hasn't sunk in yet. Undoubtedly, it's the greatest moment in my life and it was one of my main ambitions to win the British Open. I never thought it would come this soon and I feel very grateful that it has.

'It makes all the travelling I have done over the past couple of years, to the States and elsewhere, worthwhile. Just a few weeks ago in America I missed five cuts in six weeks and I got to the stage where I thought, will I ever play well again? I said to my wife, book us on a plane and let's get out.

'I must continue to play in America, as I believe it has helped me tremendously in winning here. The experience of playing for all that money every week and the keen competition was partly responsible for my win. I don't think the game would have stood up to the pressure without that experience.'

LEE TREVINO after the third round of the 1971 Open Championship at Royal Birkdale, when he led by one shot from Tony Jacklin and Liang Huan Lu (Mr Lu) and after winning:

L. Trevino	69, 70, 69, 70 – 278
Liang Huan Lu	70, 70, 69, 70 – 279
A. Jacklin	69, 70, 70, 71 – 280

'I made too many mistakes: I shouldn't be in the lead. I had four bogeys and eight birdies. I was making bogeys on the easy holes, making bogeys with my putter, which is the club that usually saves me. I feel very confident because I'm striking the ball better every day. I'm working the ball and I know approximately what it is going to do. I'm getting used to the bounces on the greens. If I can eliminate the bogeys tomorrow, or make no more than two, then my chances of winning are exceptionally good because I'm making so many birdies every round. I've made ten or eleven bogeys in three rounds and I'm eleven under par, which means I'm striking the ball well.

'You won't believe this – I played with Mr Lu in 1959. He was in the National Chinese Air Force in Taiwan and we used to take a team from Okinawa to play them. I was beaten by him by eight and seven on one occasion. We played a golf course like St Andrews: it had two flags on every green and I kept shooting at the wrong damned flag.

'Today, I was a little upset by the crowds on the front nine. In fact, I probably said a lot of things I should not have said. But that's just the way I am: I get mad. In any business or sport if you don't get mad, you have no drive. I get mad and it makes me play better.

'I believe if a man makes a bad shot or three putts, a crowd should not say anything. When I missed a putt on the sixth they cheered and clapped, and then I bogied the seventh and they cheered again. I three-putted the eighth and they really went wild and I felt like going up in the gallery with my putter.

'When you get a gallery as big as we have here, I'd be the last to say anything, because I realize that without those people coming in and spending their two pounds to watch us play we would be playing for a trophy, not for money. I'm not one to criticize a crowd, I know what they've done for me. But I'd like to say I think it is very rude to cheer someone who misses a golf shot. You feel bad enough as it is. You wouldn't get that in the crowds in America – they feel for you.

'I know it's difficult because I was playing with Tony (Jacklin) today, but I was very upset for a while.'

LEE TREVINO after winning:
'Fantastic. I don't know what to say. This is one I've always wanted. I didn't feel any pressure out there today. I went out and

one-putted the first six greens and a man who feels pressure doesn't do that. The crowds were beautiful. I've won three major titles in four weeks [US Open, Canadian Open]. The secret? I really don't know; it's just the way I play golf.'

JACK NICKLAUS after winning the 1978 Open Championship at St Andrews:

J. Nicklaus	71, 72, 69, 69 – 281
B. Crenshaw	70, 69, 73, 71 – 283
R. Floyd	69, 75, 71, 68 – 283
T. Kite	72, 69, 72, 70 – 283
S. Owen	70, 75, 67, 71 – 283
P. Oosterhuis	72, 70, 69, 73 – 284

'It feels super, the feeling of winning at St Andrews, not having won a major for almost three years and not having played particularly well this year even though I have scored well. Probably I played the best tournament from tee to green I have ever played. I have never hit the ball so solidly and consistently shot after shot.

'I am very proud of myself for being able to do what I did, what I had to do, I feel great about it. You get unhappy with yourself when you can't really perform and several times this year I've had chances to win and done some dumb thing.

'In many ways it is one of my most satisfying victories and at least for a while I haven't got to answer the question of why haven't I won a major in three years. I've now won seventeen majors, three British Opens, and every time you win one it's a great thrill. It's pretty hard to pick one that means more than another, but right now I feel great and each one of them has felt great.

'It has occurred to me that I might never win another major – you guys ask me often enough. There's always the question, will you ever win anything again? I feel now I'm a better player than I've ever been, more patient, very composed and I control my nerves a lot better as I get older. I'm not as strong and I can't overpower a golf course any more, although I am still plenty long. You do wonder, am I slipping or is it a figment of my imagination? The thought is always there. I've always considered if I continue to work at it, to play well, then I'll win several more.'

So near and yet so far

ALAN BOOTH

The world, it's said, remembers only winners. Occasionally, though, a thought is spared for the ones who came second. Sympathy flowed for Doug Sanders when he missed that three-foot putt on the last green in the 1970 Open at St Andrews and let in Jack Nicklaus to win the play-off the next day. Ed Sneed's failure in the 1979 US Masters, too, brought him plenty of commiserations, which can be little consolation in the aftermath of defeat.

Zoeller won, but it was more than a Masters that Sneed lost. If Lady Luck was handing out favours that day they certainly didn't go the way of Sneed, a thirty-four-year-old Virginian who had been encouraged to become a tournament player by his friend Tom Weiskopf, like him a product of Ohio State University. And on that fluctuating last day, amid the glories of Augusta, another former Buckeye was to play some part in piling on the pressure which ultimately destroyed Sneed. He was Jack Nicklaus.

No one really thought Sneed could lose as the final round began. He had been in command almost from the start, and was only a stroke behind Bruce Lietzke on the first day. At half-way, Sneed was in the lead jointly with Craig Stadler, three strokes clear of the field, and after three rounds Sneed had surged in front. He was five shots to the good and no one in the history of the Masters had ever lost such a lead on the final day. There was no disputing that Sneed had taken control of the tournament. Yet after nine holes, Watson had moved within two strokes, Zoeller within four and Nicklaus five. When his lead over Watson and Nicklaus had narrowed to a single stroke, Sneed was in trouble. But he responded well, resisting the pressure by picking up two more birdies and, with three holes to play, was three strokes ahead of Watson and Zoeller, four ahead of Nicklaus.

Then, with the pressure gone, Sneed let it slip, three-putting at the sixteenth and seventeenth. Of the final drama at the eighteenth, he recalls: 'I am not saying this as an alibi or crying over it, but I hit a couple of decent shots at the eighteenth, which people don't realize. On my second shot, the ball bounced to the right five or six yards, when it should have bounced left. It finished on the brink of the right-hand bunker, sitting half in and half out, and I hit a good shot. If I had lost my composure, the shot there would have shown it. I pitched to six feet and hit a pretty decent putt. I thought it would break to the right and it hung to the left and still caught the edge of the hole and I thought it was going to drop. I guess it was not meant to be.'

At the second extra hole of the play-off Sneed, whose ball had run into a bunker at the back of the green, almost holed with a remarkable effort. Watson from fifteen feet left the ball an inch short, and Zoeller stroked the ball home from eight feet, and hurled his putter high into the air – he had become the first player since Gene Sarazen in 1935, the second year of the Masters, to win on his first appearance.

A sad Sneed had no excuses, except to maintain that it wasn't a tournament that he had blown – it was one that got away. 'I had played better and with more confidence than ever before. I never felt the tournament slipping away and I never doubted myself,' he said.

'The Masters was the big tournament I should have won, but didn't. I can't honestly say whether it was the result of a breakdown in concentration or whether it was a putting failure. I think putting has hurt me some over the years – it certainly cost me the Masters.'

It was many months later before he could bring himself to talk at length about how the shock of losing a title he never doubted he was going to win had affected his life and his golf.

'I've relived it many times, but I refuse to dwell on it and spend the rest of my life thinking about it,' he told me. 'It's something I'll always remember, but I refuse to let it get me down. I didn't play any of my shots badly over those last three holes, and it was eight days later when someone sent me a videotape of the tournament and I saw Watson hit it into the trees at eighteen and Zoeller hit his second shot fat. I never hit any shots like that, yet they all talk about how I succumbed to the pressure. That's not true.

'What disappoints me most when I think about the tournament is that it really was my week. I had the tournament in hand from the second round on and I knew I was going to win right from the start. It was one of those weeks when you feel that way. Once in a while you seem to have command of all the shots and it seems impossible not to win, for you know your game is right. It will always be one I should have won. If I win it in the future, as I think I can, I dare say I won't win it in the way that I could have done that day.'

Not surprisingly, Sneed suffered from the effects of the disappointment and the shock. 'A tremendous amount of reaction set in. I continued to play well afterwards, and the lessons I learned will help me win again. I know I'm going to have the chance to win a big tournament again and, when I do, I'll have learned from my experience.'

When the day comes, and surely it must, it will be a victory Sneed will have earned.

Love-hate talk in the Press tent

JOHN INGHAM *Sports Council*

These days they impose fines on British professionals for saying anything remotely critical about a golf course, even though it may be a frightful goat track. It is a waste of time for the press to ask players what they think about a course because few of them can afford opinions like the one alleged to have been expressed by Gary Player about St Andrews, the Home of Golf: 'It should be towed out to sea and sunk!'

Comments from diplomatic winners are noted, but seldom remembered. American Curtis Strange, after collecting a fistful of dollars at the Westchester Classic, made the writers uneasy by saying that years from then when the money was spent he would think about his win. 'Memories will be my real winnings, my real happiness.' Cynical reporters said 'Gosh!'

Reporting golf has changed completely in the last thirty years. Now we have TV sets in the press room, mechanical aids such as computers to calculate what score should qualify, and press conferences with a microphone and a Press Officer who asks the star a question if we reporters dry up.

When I was young, you interviewed golfers at the nineteenth hole if you had an expense account, or around the loo area if you hadn't. Scores were put up on a blackboard and at that time famous old Prestwick became infamous because its officials said they didn't want the press chaps in the clubhouse. Only a protest from the sponsors, frightened at walk-out threats by Leonard Crawley, got us inside, where we ate dry sandwiches.

There are now two types of pressman covering the sport: the golf regulars with a metal Association badge, and the much-feared wandering newshound after headlines, no matter who gets hurt. This fellow helps create the occasional rumpus and regards the specialist sports writer as a failed news gatherer.

At Wimbledon tennis competitors are fined if they refuse to attend the after-match press conference, and this compulsion is necessary because beaten players often sulk or fear that they might blurt out the opinion that the umpire is a bum. In my experience golf competitors willingly talk, but do not always answer every question. Arnold Palmer is a master of the non-answer, particularly if unfamiliar reporters are around. Then he may clam up entirely. When he turned totally silent (about long grass in a free-drop zone at Sandwich, Kent) I knew for sure that things had changed. His dread was that the press might quote him saying something disparaging about the Royal and Ancient organizers. So, fearing headlines, he sat stubbornly silent.

In the old days the professionals called Bernard Darwin 'Sir' and never argued the toss, just as long as their names were spelled correctly. Things had changed by 1962 when Jack Nicklaus made a midnight visit to my room in the Marine Hotel, Troon, to complain that I had quoted him on why the Brits were no good at golf. His theory had been that we drink too much tea and ate overcooked cabbage. 'But I was telling *you*,' he moaned, 'not Fleet Street!' So we developed off-the-record chats and it took me some time to dare to cross-examine him at any public press conferences.

After following golf for many years, I find there are few players worthy of hero-worship. Pettiness is too obvious, tunnel-vision of the so-called stars too boring. I never want an autograph and don't expect a great speech or brilliant thinking from golfing winners, but so many players have so little to say and then you realize the awful truth: their whole existence and experience in life has occurred on the golf course.

Some even pretend to avoid the press. 'They misquote you dreadfully,' they say, like some poor man's Noël Coward. But we find that they won't stop talking and, like Max Faulkner, are prepared to say anything that will get them into print.

So, with this background, and with a slight sense of mischief, I was compelled to ask the greatest golfer the world has ever seen how he celebrates a success. Does he pop a champagne cork or do anything dramatic? For the record, the greatest display of emotion from Nicklaus came at St Andrews when he actually threw his putter in the air and it nearly fell on Doug Sanders, the man he had just beaten in a play-off.

Anyway, Jack told me he doesn't like champagne, sees no sense in getting drunk, and enjoys being with Barbara and the children and, if the occasion demands, he takes them down the road and they buy hamburgers. 'But what will you do when you win your twentieth major championship or your twenty-first?' I asked, feeling he just might admit to something fresh and exciting.

'Just to be with my family, that's the best celebration for me.'

For some journalists, this isn't enough. They want a memorable quote, a hard news angle to satisfy the editor. And, ideally, they want their story on page one. Desperately they try to keep a top golfer afloat with ideas, or they sometimes even invent a quote and ask him if he agrees. But the plain truth is that most golfers can only talk about their clubs and after bagging birdies are drained of all else.

So, in desperation, do you wonder that some cheeky writer dared ask Greg Norman whether it is true he dyes his hair to become a Jack Nicklaus look-alike? It isn't, but the question *was* asked.

After that, what can we expect next? The mind boggles.

Chocks away for Greg Norman

MITCHELL PLATTS   *Golf World*

In the time it takes Greg Norman to inhale one deep breath before striking a golf ball, he could have been lost to the professional golfing world.

At the age of nineteen, with pen poised to confirm a career in the Royal Australian Air Force as a fighter pilot, Norman made the decision that was to change his life. He refused to sign.

After two years of training, Norman sat with his father on one side and his squadron-leader on the other. He had done his training, had passed all the exams. He had been accepted.

Now, as father looked on proudly, all Greg had to do was sign the piece of paper that had been placed in front of him. 'Nope.' That was all Norman said. 'Nope.'

Norman, recalling the moment, explained: 'I looked at that piece of paper and I told myself "Don't sign it". I told myself "Go and play golf".'

'If I had signed I would never have played golf. Sure, there would have been some social stuff sometime later, but that's all. Once I had signed that piece of paper, my clubs would have been laid to rest for five years. I had done two years of training on the academic side, and I would have had three years of practical work ahead of me. And once I had got my full fighter pilot's licence I would have been flying all the time. Golf would have been gone. So a few seconds across that table swung my life – and I haven't a regret!'

The lifeline which took Norman to within a whisker of spending his time in the air with the birds rather than making birdies (and eagles) on the ground began in Mount Isa, Australia's biggest mining city. His father worked for a mining company, but three months after Greg was born the family moved to Townsville, some 800 miles away, where Mr Norman set up his own engineering company.

At school, first at Townsville Grammar School and later at High School in Brisbane, Norman established himself as an all-round sportsman. He played cricket, reaching State level by representing Queensland, Australian Rules football, and Rugby League. He became a strong swimmer, and in athletics, over 440 yards, he was robust and successful. 'I enjoyed Australian Rules most; it's fast, exciting and it never stops. I went off Rugby League when I was sixteen, when I got a bad kick in the head.'

Ironically, as if to replace a lost sport from his busy schedule, it was at the age of sixteen years and eight months that Norman turned to golf. It was triggered by his parents' moving again – this time from Townsville to Brisbane. 'I didn't know anybody. My mother was a three-handicap golfer, she plays off five now, and she was keen to get started at a new club – the Virginia Golf Club in Brisbane. She went down to play; I went to caddy for her.

'When the round was over I borrowed her clubs just for a few hits. I must have hit a couple of good shots. I thought it was a good game and that was it. I got a basic set of 3–5–7–9 putter and three wood and taught myself after school. After six months, and with my handicap coming down fast, my father bought me my first full set of clubs and a pair of spiked shoes. I was still playing Australian Rules and squash to keep fit, but golf was taking over. I got down to scratch in twenty months – which, certainly in Australia, was pretty fast.'

Norman's progress was rewarded by the Virginia Golf Club. They presented him with a special award for reaching scratch status so quickly.

It was virtually impossible to keep Greg off the golf course. The only time he got away from golf was when the family went to their holiday house on the Great Barrier Reef, where Greg joined the beach life-saving school.

'But most of the time it was golf, golf, golf. I would get out there on the course before school, as the sun was coming up, and go back after school until the sun went down. The practice area at Virginia was not particularly big and so I also joined Royal Queensland, courtesy of my father paying the fees, and at weekends you couldn't get me away from the place. I practised every day for eight hours, and I mean eight hours.'

Although the furthest Norman ever made as an amateur was to represent Queensland and reach the quarter-finals of the Australian Amateur – in which he was beaten by Terry Gale – it was clear that he had the potential to become a fine golfer. When he turned down the Air Force, it took him only a few months to become a professional.

'There isn't much to stay amateur for in Australia, no Walker Cup or anything like that. I figured that as I was so keen on the game and I was determined to do well at it, I might as well turn professional sooner rather than later.'

Norman ran straight into controversy. 'As a trainee pro in Australia you had to wait three years before you could go out and play in a tournament. But that was in Queensland. In New South Wales they had a different set of rules which basically defined that if you could pass the full examination course you could go out and get invited as a national trainee. So I went down to Sydney. I passed all the exams in six months. That was the quickest on record – and then I went along and won my player's card. I was ready to try and get an invitation as a national trainee, but they bluntly told me: "We're not going to let you play." They didn't give a reason.

'I got on the phone back home to Charlie Earp, my first teacher, and he told me to go back and work for him. He said he would do what he could. That was in June, 1976. I worked for him for two months, and then I received six invitations to national events. Charlie fixed it all for me.'

Norman didn't let Charlie or himself down. In his first event, the South Coast Open, he finished joint fourth. Next week he hit sixty-two of the seventy-two greens in regulation figures to finish joint third in the Queensland Open. He had to settle for a share of the thirteenth place seven days later behind Jack Newton in the New South Wales Open.

The following week, in the West Lakes Classic in Adelaide, Greg Norman became a winner. The field included David Graham, Graham Marsh, Bruce Devlin, Billy Dunk, Bruce Crampton and Jack Newton. But the golf establishment knew they had a rival when Norman covered the first nine holes at the Grange Golf Club in thirty-one shots. Peter Thomson, five times winner of the Open, joined the gallery that cheered Norman along the back stretch to an opening sixty-four – four strokes better than anybody else.

Norman added 67 and 66 to that opening 64 to forge a full ten shots clear. It didn't matter that he took 74 in the last round. His final winning margin was five shots – and Greg Norman had arrived.

'The pressure hit me on the final day. The first three days I just played golf. I just tried to knock the flags out. Then I realized what was going on. I was really nervous over the last six holes. The pressure that day was so different to the pressure one experiences now. I know now what I've done. I know I've won. The positions I get in now have probably been duplicated before. So it's a lot easier. But it was tough that last day at Adelaide, although I really enjoyed it.'

The comparisons with Jack Nicklaus began less than a week later. It had not so much to do with style, looks, build or mannerisms, but with a little bit of 'rigging'. It was the Australian Open and Norman was paired with Nicklaus for the first two holes. It wasn't a great start for Norman. He came down to earth with a bump and an 80. But it was a great honour and being paired with Nicklaus so early in his professional life gave Norman further incentive to strive for the top.

Norman's rapid success created a dilemma for the Australians over the World Cup. 'I had accumulated enough points to be selected, but trainees weren't allowed. A swift change of the rules got me to Los Angeles in December.'

In 1977 Norman set out on a career as an international player, winning the Kusaha Invitational in Japan and the Martini International at Blairgowrie, Scotland, where a last round of 66 enabled him to sprint past his rivals. That ability to put in a hot finish became a Greg Norman trademark, as he showed again in the Martini International in 1981, when he finished birdie-eagle on Wentworth's 'Burma Road' to snatch another glorious victory. It was his sixteenth win since the West Lakes Classic, but it was his triumph in the Suntory World Match Play Championship at Wentworth seven months earlier which really launched him as an international star.

'I was confident until then, but my attitude began to change with my win in the World Match Play Championship. You get to know all the big name players as you go along the trail, but it's difficult to tell yourself you can beat them. The World Match Play started a new feeling. Winning the Australian Open kept that feeling going. Coming fourth in the 1981 US Masters was final proof. Once I realized how many players I had beaten on a tough golf course, it did bundles for me psychologically.

'I knew then that there was only one target – to be the best. I had thought about it time and time again, turned it over in my mind. But now I was certain. I was certain that I had the ability to be the number one golfer in the world: and that is what I'm going to be.'

Bang goes ten million bucks

ALISTER NICOL   *Daily Record*

There's not a lot about Lee Trevino that could be described as ordinary. His swing is unique, his sense of humour and fair play are as legendary as his wonderful talent for manufacturing shots, and his rags-to-riches life story is a mirror of the American Dream.

Lee Trevino is in fact an extraordinary man. But the story he related to me late in 1980 was the most sensational sporting tale I've ever heard. And, typical of Trevino, it had to be told in some exotic spot – the Rabat Hilton in Morocco to be precise.

It had taken me the best part of nine months and something approaching 25,000 miles to convince the normally-voluble Super Mex that his weird and far-from-wonderful tale was one that ought to be recorded – if only as a warning to other sportsmen to be wary of the financial minefields lurking in wait for the unwary or ill-advised.

It all began back in 1967 when Lee and his wife Claudia moved out from the driving range at which he'd been working in Dallas to a new complex called Horizon Hills in El Paso.

'I recall we had fifty dollars between us,' said Lee. 'And my job at the club entailed me working in the pro shop in the mornings, for which the owners of the club, brothers called Don and Jesse Whittington, paid me between thirty and forty dollars.

'But in the afternoons I'd practise and go out and play big-money games with the gamblers. I won a few bucks.'

Then in the June of that year the Whittingtons lent Lee $400 to go the US Open at Baltusrol. Lee finished fifth, won $6000 and the road to fame and fortune suddenly opened up.

Into the picture stepped a colourful character called Bucky Woy, a fast-talking wheeler-dealer with a penchant for stetsons and high-heeled cowboy boots.

'The Whittingtons suggested I get me a manager so we employed Bucky – briefly,' said Lee. 'One day I found out that while Bucky was getting me nice fat contracts he was also working little side deals for himself.

'When I found out about that I told Bucky he'd have to go and that little episode cost me 168,000 dollars to be paid over eighteen months. But, you know, Bucky was the kind of guy who just could not stop. I read in an Akron paper a few days later that Bucky claimed his settlement was 500,000.'

Within a year Lee had won the US Open and millionaire status was his for the taking. He made money, lots of it. He bought 160 apartments, he paid plenty for a couple of acres of land in downtown El Paso, he and Claudia built a dream home costing $300,000, and he thought he owned a part-share in the thirty-six-hole Santa Teresa complex.

For the next eight years Trevino went on winning tournaments and friends all over the world, happy in the knowledge that he was also becoming a very wealthy man.

But there was one person who was unhappy. Claudia. For years she kept telling Lee she suspected all was not well with their financial status. But for years he did not listen. In January 1976 it finally got through to Lee when Claudia called him up in Tucson, Arizona, to tell him tearfully that she was quitting her dream home in El Paso and going back to Dallas because the bank would not tell her how much she and her husband owned.

'It transpired that instead of the club making me money I was paying back 400,000 a year in interest alone,' Lee went on, shaking his head. 'Don Whittington had put up my home as collateral, my contracts, my apartments, my two acres of land, even my life insurance policies. I owned nothing. They had me lock, stock and barrel.

'So I called Donnie and told him to arrange a meeting with all the lawyers and accountants and I went along with my own lawyer, a little Jewish fellow whom I'd been raised with in Dallas.

When I insisted I was finished with the whole deal, that I was getting out, one banker just kinda looked at me said, "We have everything you own as collateral."

'And my reply to him was this. I said: "The collateral is worth only as much as that piece of paper in your hand. Because, mister, you can't get blood out of a turnip. And one thing you cannot control is my putting. If you look at those contracts you will find they all have performance clauses written in to them. And from now on if I want to I can three-putt every green I step on".'

The bankers and lawyers told Lee he owed them $1.5 million and he retorted that the assets at the club alone were worth $400 million. The wrangling went on for two more years before it was finally cleared up and Trevino emerged a sadder, poorer but much wiser man.

'I suppose in cash terms I was burned for maybe one and a half million. But, heck, the late sixties and early seventies were my prime earning years, and, with the amount of cash I was making then, I could have bought into all sorts of investments. I guess you could say that the deal cost me ten million dollars. That's not to say I lost ten million – just that I would have been ten million better off. And that's a lot of money in anybody's terms. I was just too trusting, I suppose. I loved those Whittingtons like brothers.'

It is a frightening tale in many respects but Trevino has put it all behind him now. He can earn around two million dollars a year, he's building more property in Dallas and he's banking a tidy sum each week. He'll never be poor. But he'll never be caught again.

A zest for life

RICHARD DODD   *Yorkshire Post*

Life has been good to the man they call Queenie. He drives a 140 m.p.h. Porsche, wines and dines at the best restaurants, always stays at a Hilton when he's abroad, and is invited to the smartest parties in and around his home base of Sunningdale, a beautiful corner of Surrey.

Queenie is eloquent and elegant, six feet two inches tall with striking good looks and sun-bleached hair. He is a decidedly snappy dresser with a penchant for champagne and blondes, although not necessarily in that order, and his generally extravagant life-style is financed through his deeds on the golf course and occasional raids on the stock market.

Queenie is Michael King, an ex-public schoolboy, ex-window cleaner, ex-bricklayer and ex-stockbroker who now earns a substantial crust as a professional golfer. He is well rewarded for his efforts on the course but even after several years as a professional he still regards golf as just a game. The whole of life is just a game, he says, and he is getting all the fun he can while it lasts.

The nickname of Queenie has been with Mike King since his days as a leading amateur golfer and he does not object in the least to being so called. Rather the opposite. He quite enjoys it and says: 'Take my word for it, I'm no poof.'

A more apt description would be playboy, a role he has has been pursuing since he was a noisy four-year-old hacking his way round Reading golf course with his mother's set of lightweight clubs. He was a golfing prodigy, beating astonished senior members to take the golf club championship at the age of fourteen and attaining a scratch handicap when he was fifteen.

At that time his father packed him off to Britain's most famous sporting public school, Millfield, where King's liking for the good life and the necessary cash to finance it began to develop. He has often had to live by his wits and the good offices of his bank manager but he has always surfaced from minor financial skirmishes smelling of roses – and still smiling.

King was forced into professional golf in the mid 1970s because of the precarious state of the stock market (he describes it as a crash) and has not regretted one moment of his new sporting career. Indeed, it has enabled him to lead an even more extravagant life than when he toured the jolly amateur circuit for six years. Those who know him well say he is still an amateur at heart and he says his happiest times away from the PGA European tour are playing friendly games at his beloved Sunningdale Golf Club.

By 'friendly' he means sidestakes of up to £100 a corner, which in that part of Surrey is neither excessive nor bankrupting. 'It costs me between £300 and £500 a week to play golf so I should be able to back myself to beat another fellow for £100,' he says. 'I used to gamble a lot in my amateur days, often more than I could afford to lose. I'm not saying it was right but that was me . . . and it didn't do me much harm.'

Michael King's father, an established and respected estate agent, was a one-handicap golfer and the youngest captain of the Reading Golf Club back in 1964. It was he who taught the infant Queenie the rudiments of the game, and the other club members encouraged the fair-haired and personable child when they spotted his natural flair.

Although King achieved national standards at swimming, played soccer for Reading Schoolboys and Rugby Union for Berkshire Schools, it was golf which became his passionate interest.

The young Queenie established himself as a gifted player while at Millfield, captaining both the England boys' and youths' teams; and within a year of leaving school had become a member of the senior England side. His first year as a non-schoolboy was spent playing full-time amateur golf, financed by unstylish spells – for him – as a window cleaner and bricklayer. And he soon acquired a taste for the good life.

The next move was to raise the funds to pay competition entry fees, caddies, motoring bills, hotel bills, restaurant bills and wine bills. He decided to become a stockbroker.

'I was not born with the proverbial silver spoon in my mouth as some people thought,' says King, 'and I went into stockbroking because I thought it was a good way to make money if you knew a few people and had a modicum of intelligence. I trained with a firm and then joined up with my best friend, working for my own clients.

'I started with an overdraft and made quite a lot of money. And I lost it just as quick. It was one of life's great lessons and I'm still learning it.'

King still goes in for some audacious calculated investments (share gambling to us) on the stock market, winning a few and losing a few. 'Money comes and goes and at the end of the day I don't seem to be any richer or poorer. I have a lot of fun out of it but I once lost more on one share dealing than the amount I could have won for a major tournament victory. It's a bit depressing when you lose a few thousand but I'm not scared to have another go because I'm a genuine investor and I like the business.'

King's excursion into professional golf has been spectacularly successful and he still appears to spend as much as he earns. He estimates it costs him £15,000 a year in expenses; and he says with a slight look of bewilderment: 'I don't seem to be able to spend any less.'

The transition from the play-for-fun amateur days of golf and gins and tonics to the harsh play-for-pay professional ranks was not easy. 'I thought it would be jolly difficult and sure enough it was. The most difficult part of the transition was having so much spare time. Playing golf was all right for five hours a day but what do you do with the other nineteen? I can't sleep that long.'

King's first tilt at the professional game in 1975 earned him a meagre £541, but since then he has progressed rapidly and is regarded by his fellow professionals as a player of outstanding ability. Within four seasons of leaving the Stock Exchange he had won a major title, the European Tournament Players' Championship, and had been selected for the Ryder Cup team, thus becoming one of the few players to represent Great Britain and Ireland at the highest levels of both amateur and professional golf.

At a recent end-of-season tournament, early morning fog disrupted play on the final day and eventually forced officials to reduce the size of the field in order to complete the event on time. Those who were asked to stand down included Michael King. He and a group of his friends were sitting disconsolately in a corner bemoaning the fact that fog had prevented them climbing higher up the £100,000 prize list – when King eased himself out of his chair, strode purposefully to the bar and beckoned a well-built waitress.

'Darling, we're all terribly depressed,' he told her. 'A bottle of Moët and Chandon, if you please.'

As the champagne flowed the depression lifted. And the size of the party grew.

Queenie, still smiling his way through the disappointment of not playing in the final round, invited me to join in, saying: 'As I was saying, I don't seem to be able to spend any less . . .'

PART FOUR

For amusement only

'Play away, Mr Wodehouse, please'

RAYMOND JACOBS *Glasgow Herald*

There should be an air of rejoicing in the Elysian Fields Golf and Country Club. The first appearance of a new member as distinguished as P. G. Wodehouse will not readily be ignored even at an establishment that has already welcomed so many of the great men of the game across its threshold.

The brass name-plate will have been attached to his locker door, stocks of his favourite pipe tobacco laid in, and the barman will be wiping the cocktail glasses with a livelier wipe. Outside, similar preparations will be well in hand.

The professional and his assistant will be waiting respectfully at the entrance to the shop. The caddy master will be casting a thoughtful and piercing eye over the ranks of angelic faces as he weighs up a suitable candidate. The starter in his box by the first tee will have pencilled in a favourable time.

Undoubtedly the weather, like yesterday and tomorrow, will be perfect – the sort of morning when, as Wodehouse began one of his inimitable stories, 'all Nature shouted "Fore"'. The Oldest Member will surely be in attendance on the clubhouse veranda, but the Wrecking Crew, the undoing of many an enjoyable round, will have been warned off.

This imaginary scenario has its roots in the truth of the game –

'That varied never-ending pageant that men call golf' – as Wodehouse saw it. He wrote of it, as he did in his major novels, as a world which, as someone perceptively observed 'stopped on Boat Race night of the year of the Relief of Mafeking'.

More accurately, it never really existed at all, except in the author's unique and fertile imagination. As with Bertie Wooster, Jeeves, Barmy Fotheringay-Phipps, and Looney Coote, so with golf. For Gussie Fink-Nottle, after his orange juice had been liberally spiked with gin, the world was a beautiful place – and so, with few exceptions, it was, too, for golfers.

All the same, Wodehouse's golf stories contain instantly recognizable situations, emotions, and characters. The severe critic might say that the plots are repetitious, for invariably they have to do with some tangled affair of the heart. But one does not read them for an insight into life's deeper meaning, rather for the dazzling virtuosity of the verbal style.

Yet frequently the two come together, as in 'It is one of the chief merits of golf that non-success at the game induces a certain amount of decent humility. I attribute the insane arrogance of the later Roman emperors entirely to the fact that, having never played golf, they never knew that strange chastening humility which is engendered by a topped chip shot.'

Or again – 'If Cleopatra had been ousted in the first round of the Ladies' Singles we should have heard a lot less of her proud imperiousness.' Come to that, Wodehouse also laid down – 'There are higher, nobler things than love. A woman is only a woman, but a hefty drive is a slosh.'

Like most of us Wodehouse took to golf rather more than it took to him. In his preface to *The Golf Omnibus* he confessed: 'I won my first and only trophy, a striped umbrella, in a hotel tournament in Aiken, South Carolina, where, hitting them squarely on the meat for once, I went through a field of some of the fattest retired business men in America like a devouring flame.'

Wodehouse was a master of the telling phrase and the apt metaphor. In golf, as in his 'lay' stories, he has made countless felicitous contributions to the grammar of the game. He described the man who 'missed short putts because of the uproar of the butterflies in the adjoining meadows' and another 'who never spared himself in his efforts to do it (the ball) a violent injury'.

Relief, as Wodehouse describes it, can be compared with a golfer who 'sees his ball heading for dense rough, only to hit a rock and rebound on to the fairway'. One hero satisfactorily concludes a romance by folding the adored one in his arms 'using the interlocking grip' and a heroine, a heretic converted to golf, is only dissuaded by earnest pleading from christening her first-born Abe Mitchell Rib-Faced Mashie Banks.

If it is true that the world is divided into those who cannot stand Wodehouse's style – which is their bad luck – and those whose devotion is like that perfect peace, the peace that passeth all understanding, it will by now be obvious on which side of the line I stand. I was educated in the finer lunacies of the game by reading Wodehouse.

The astonishing thing is that Wodehouse wrote all his golf stories between fifty and sixty years ago. His terminology gives that fact away. Yet they are timeless and the essence of them is as strong today as it was then. When his daughter died suddenly he was moved to say: 'I thought she was immortal.' His writing will certainly always remain so.

And now if that apostle on the right will kindly stand back a little – 'Play away, Mr Wodehouse, please.'

The kid from the flea pit

RON WILLS   *Daily Mirror*

Taking a right-hander in the chops from Muhammad Ali or Joe Frazier isn't many people's idea of a fun way to spend an evening. But there was a time when Henry Cooper might have preferred that to waiting to hit his opening tee shot of the day in a pro-am golf tournament.

Happily for Henry, those days are now over. But the confident-looking eight-handicapper who is now one of the amateur 'regulars' on the British pro-am circuit went through nightmares, suffered embarrassments and lost countless hours of sleep when he first dabbled in golf with the professionals.

The mis-hit drive, the movement you didn't really mean to make which put your pro partner off his awkward six-foot putt and cost him money, the fluffed pitch into a bunker after your pro had just spent three minutes telling you precisely how to play the shot to avoid it, those little nervous twitches on the green which relegate your team from joint second to fifth place and out of the prizes – Henry, like us all, has suffered them all. And as with all of us amateurs, mistakes can still creep into Henry's game. But compared to his first toe-in-the-water of pro-am golf they are now few and far between.

Henry first took up golf – in spite of himself – about eleven years ago, shortly before he retired from boxing in 1971. Before that, though, he had a quite different view of the game. He explained: 'I used to watch all sport on television, and when golf came on I just couldn't make out why people were so interested. It seemed such a daft game to me – and I used to think what a silly lot of so-and-so's they are chasing a little white ball all over the place.'

By the time his career came to an end, a career which included holding the British, European and Commonwealth heavyweight titles – and the satisfaction of dumping the then brash Cassius Clay on the seat of his pants – Henry's views on the game have changed. 'I started playing about a year or so before I finished boxing, and I was soon cured of my earlier views. By the time my handicap was down to nineteen I was hooked on the game. I played three or four times a week – I still do. Now I'm down to eight, but I can't see my handicap getting any lower.'

Henry's first venture into pro-am golf came at Royal Mid-Surrey when he played in the old Bowmaker thirty-six-hole competition, and he found himself partnering former Open Champion Kel Nagle of Australia. And on the first tee, Henry suffered all the pains and doubts and fears that strike terror into the heart of every amateur on his first big occasion.

Said Henry: 'I was sweating up. I could feel my legs trembling like I'd just been hit by a perfect left hook, and the palms of my hands were moist. I tell you something, I don't think I ever felt as nervous as I did that day before any of my fights, whether they were championship fights or stepping into the ring with Ali.

'The crowd didn't help, either. At the first hole before I played my opening tee shot, I shouted out asking for them to move back. I was scared stiff I was going to hit someone. But instead of moving, they just laughed. They thought it was my idea of a joke.'

Incredibly, Henry recalls, he and Kel Nagle led after the opening eighteen holes. 'I went home feeling like Arnold Palmer. But the nerves were still with me. I couldn't sleep all night, I was so excited.' But it was no story-book ending. 'The next day I played like a drain and we finished nowhere.'

There have been some nasty and embarrassing moments on the course for Henry, too. Once, during a pro-am that was being filmed by BBC2, one of his drives flew right and struck a BBC continuity girl on the chest. Fortunately she wasn't badly hurt, but he recalls: 'It upset me a hell of a lot, and I just couldn't play anything like my normal game for the rest of the day.' Then there was the pro-am when he strode on to the course in his golfing trousers which were freshly back from the cleaners. When he bent down to line up a putt the stitching in the trousers split in a most unfortunate place. 'I didn't have a clue what to do,' says Henry. 'But about thirty women round the green rushed forward offering safety pins.'

As Henry's handicap dropped, so the pro-am offers flowed in with increasing regularity, and as he grew in confidence so it became somebody else's turn to be on the receiving end of embarrassing moments.

'I remember, once, playing with a very well known film star who loved to theorize about the game. We were playing with Doug Sanders, on a Scottish course, and stopped after nine holes for some drinks and food. Then this fella suddenly said: "Of course, on your American courses you American players never learned how to play the pitch and run shot that we play over here, did you?" Sanders never said a word. He just took eight or nine balls and a seven iron out of his bag and proceeded to chip and run them from off the green towards the hole. The one that finished furthest from the hole was only about eighteen inches away. Then Sanders just laughed, left his caddy to pick up the balls and walked on to the next tee. The film star didn't say another word for the rest of the round.'

Asked which pro-am has given him the most pleasure, Henry has no hesitation in answering: 'The Bob Hope – it's the ultimate. I've played in pro-ams all over the world – Kenya, the West Indies, America, all over Europe. Four days of golf with some of the best players in the world, with some of the greatest celebrities. It's marvellous. And playing four rounds off the same tees, well, it's like being a pro yourself. I was very lucky last year in the first Bob Hope British Classic – Lee Trevino and Bob Hope himself were among my partners.

'It was amazing, really. To think, when I was a snotty-nosed kid in Bellingham in South London I used to pay a tanner to get into the local flea pit – it was mis-named the "Splendid" as far as I remember – to see all his films. And now, here I am playing golf with the great man himself. It was a day I'll never forget.'

In the family style

JOHN HENNESSY   *The Times*

The story is told in the United States that at the time of the death of Bing Crosby on a Spanish golf course four years ago a disc jockey, suddenly confronted with the news and demanding from his library the first Crosby record they could lay their hands on, was startled by the opening lyrics: *'Heaven, I'm in Heaven . . .'* It must be apocryphal, because it's too good to be true and because 'Cheek to Cheek', anyway, is an Astaire number.

But true or not, Bing must have been in heaven, probably his seventh heaven, beaming down on the misty San Francisco Olympic Club's golf courses during the week of the United States

Amateur championship in September 1981. Golf nut that he was, and former challenger for both the US and British amateur titles, he must have been overjoyed to follow from his lofty perch the progress of his nineteen-year-old son Nathaniel to this pinnacle of his golfing career; and to see the immense reserves of character he showed when it came to the crunch in both the semi-final and final.

It was, to use the show-biz metaphor, like *The Perils of Pauline* with muscles, as young Crosby came back twice from what looked like certain defeat. In the semi-final against Willie Wood, a more elegant golfer and himself a man of courage, he recovered from three down to kill off his man with stunning bunker shots at the last three holes. He laid the first two dead and was only five feet from the hole at the treacherous eighteenth when his opponent surrendered – his spirit as well as his game, I suspected, broken beyond repair.

In the final against Brian Lindley, a man of Yorkshire antecedence, Crosby went to lunch one down and was four down by the seventh in the afternoon. From that point he played twelve holes in two under par (70) to win with a birdie at the first extra hole. This on a course – the Lakeland, as opposed to the easier Ocean – that had humiliated some of the best amateur players in the world, including members of both Walker Cup teams of the previous week. Facing a probable setback on the short fifteenth (147 yards) he followed his opponent in for a telling half in two.

Crosby has a manufactured, stilted swing which the wiseheads said would never stand the strain, but the wisest head of all, Bill Campbell, was not among them. 'I have studied his swing closely and found that it always goes into the slot up there,' he said, wielding an imaginary club to the top of the backswing. If, then, his swing was sound after all, one would look in vain for weaknesses elsewhere.

You could almost produce a Crosby musical from his various attributes – *Straight Down the Middle* for his woods and long irons: *The Touch of Your Hand*, a line from Ray Noble, for his short game: *The Road to Morocco* for his bunker play; and *How Deep is the Ocean?* for his strength of character. As for any opponent, how about *I Surrender Dear?*

There was, then, much to admire about Nathaniel Crosby, but many were offended by his aggressive attitude, bordering on manic obsession, I feared, as a fierce look came into his eye and he demonstrated with both arms pumping, fists clenched. 'Bite, ball, bite!' he would scream after a shot to the green, or otherwise command it to roll, go, kick or sit, as the occasion demanded.

Members of the United States Golf Association hierarchy shared my concern, one suggesting that the absence of paternal authority was too sadly obvious. Campbell, again, was not among them. This was normal college behaviour, he claimed (Crosby is studying political science at the University of Miami). 'I see no harm in it,' he said. I would say that Crosby behaves like a Connors rather than a McEnroe. One can see elements of Connors's fierce determination and extrovert self-galvanization in his bearing.

I have no idea what either Connors or McEnroe is like in private life, but it was a relief to meet Nathaniel Crosby a couple of times and to find him courteous and charming and aware of his responsibilities. 'It's not enough that I should be the champion,' he said at the prizegiving. 'Now I have to show that I can behave like one.'

Coming from such distinguished stock, he felt a compulsive need to make it somehow, somewhere, sometime. 'My father, my mother, my brother all made it,' he said. 'And my sister shot J. R. Gee, that's a tough act to follow.' By way of background, his mother (who followed him every step of his triumphant way) is the actress Kathy Crosby, and his sister Mary is the young lady who emerged from one of the cleverest publicity stunts of all time as the would-be assassin in *Dallas*. I'm not sure what distinction his brother holds, but did not like to ask. He may be a disc jockey.

Command performance

JOHN BAKER

One day, when I was cub sports reporter with the Press Association in the early thirties, I was in the Sports Department at Byron House, Fleet Street, with the Sports Editor. There came a rap on the office door and in walked the editor of a well known American news syndicate which occupied an office in the same building. He informed my boss that Edward, Prince of Wales was playing golf that morning at Sunningdale with the American Oxford Golf Blue, Charles Sweeny (elder brother of Bob Sweeny who was in the same Dark Blue Team as Charles and went on to win the British Amateur title).

The American editor asked if we could cover the game for them, adding, above all, a personal narrative by Sweeny on 'What it was like to play golf with the future King'. I was instructed to catch the first available train to Sunningdale.

When I arrived at the exclusive club, the first person to run an eagle-eye over me was the Prince of Wales's private detective. I hovered out of sight until the Prince and Sweeny emerged from the clubhouse to prepare themselves for the first tee. At the first available opportunity I approached Sweeny, apologized for the intrusion, introduced myself and told him what I wanted. He must have believed it a practical joke until he noticed the expression of anguish on my face.

I must point out here that at this time the Prince of Wales – an enthusiastic and keen golfer – possessed by no means a single-figure handicap, and it was strictly forbidden for the Press to follow him when playing. Believe me, his personal bodyguard saw to that. Therefore, I knew I would not be allowed on the course, and I would have to make my own assessment of the situation and let my imagination do the rest.

Sweeny, somewhat bemused by it all, was most co-operative. He told me he would speak to the Prince about the matter during their game, adding that while they were playing I would have to write the story for him and let him have it when they returned to the club. With flushed cheeks I thanked him. I found a quiet corner in the clubhouse, put myself in Sweeny's shoes and wrote my piece.

Having been despatched from Fleet Street in such a hurry I had given little thought to picking up a notebook or copy paper. All I had in my possession to scribble on were a couple of sheets of lined foolscap paper. I did have a pencil, but no pen.

The Prince and Sweeny completed their game and, seizing a moment to get Sweeny alone, I said I had written the story as he requested, apologizing at the same time for the poor presentation of the copy. 'Oh yes,' he replied, 'I've spoken to the Prince. Please let me have your story and we'll have a look at it during dinner at Fort Belvedere this evening.'

I was floored. I had imagined that Sweeny would have found a minute or two to read the story, make his own observations and any alterations he thought necessary, and let me have it back. It had never occurred to me that my copy would be a topic of conversation during a Royal meal. I came to the conclusion I would hear no more of my 'Royal Command Performance'. Reluctantly I phoned London and told my Sports Editor what had happened.

About three days later an imposing, crested buff envelope was handed into our office; and it contained my story about the Prince and Charles Sweeny. It was not the original foolscap scribble: it was now neatly typed. But apart from some modifications here and there it was very much as I had written it.

As time passed, the Prince of Wales became more than a useful golfer. One of his favourite teachers was the giant Ryder Cup pro at Coombe Hill, Archie Compston. Reporting restrictions when the Prince was playing were gradually relaxed, provided one kept out of sight as much as possible. The Prince never forgot a face and I still remember with pleasure how he would nod and pass the time of day with me on the golf course.

PART FIVE

Heroes worthy of another song

Playing the nineteenth

MIKE BRITTEN   *Exchange Telegraph*

You will not find his name in any roll of championship winners. Like the majority of amateur golfers, he plays for fun in between the demands of earning a living and raising a family. Yet for some two dozen patrons of the men's bar at Moortown Golf Club, enjoying lunchtime refreshment on a May day in 1974, he provided one of those rare cameos that are cherished long after the champion of the moment is forgotten.

It was a typical early summer morning – a warm sun dispersing the shower clouds with just enough heat to persuade the Yorkshire club members that watching the opening round of the English Stroke Play Championship was thirsty work. Then Nigel Denham, or rather the ball he struck towards the eighteenth green, burst on the convivial scene.

It should be explained that at that time the Moortown clubhouse was not out of bounds, nor was the concrete path encircling it and running alongside the eighteenth fairway and green. In golfing parlance, the whole edifice, measuring some sixty by thirty yards, was an immovable obstruction. As such it was a place to be avoided by any golfer intent on returning an unblemished medal round. Denham, a Yorkshire county player, had every intention of so doing until he struck his mid-iron to the home flag from an uphill lie, and instantly realized he had applied a vicious hook to the ball. What followed would have made a classic script for W. C. Fields.

Denham's ball bounded off the concrete path, leapt up the clubhouse steps and after cannoning off the framework of the open french windows rolled gently to rest in the centre of the bar carpet. Denham approached base with that look of desperation common to all golfers who fear impending doom. Preliminary enquiries revealed that the ball was indeed closeted indoors, and he mounted the steps in pursuit.

First there were formalities of etiquette to observe. Like most clubs, Moortown does not permit spiked shoes to be worn within its inner precincts, nor allow caddies to enter carrying the tools of their trade. The bar steward was very much a custodian of the law and if Denham wished to pass through the portals he must remove his golf shoes. Nigel complied and padded into the bar in his socks, leaving his clubs and caddy parked on the doorstep.

An expectant gallery had encircled the errant missile. Nigel surveyed it with a mixture of relief and perplexity. It was his all right – and at least the lie was perfect – indeed the carpet had been freshly cleaned. The ball was not damaged, nor was it bearing any loose impediment. There was room to swing a club, and he was still only thirty yards from the flagstick.

Denham could have ended all speculation there and then by declaring the ball unplayable, accepting a penalty stroke, and following the appropriate procedure. But a Tyke is never one to give owt for nowt, and this one needed little encouragement from the drinking gallery to be intrigued by the alternatives.

'It's an Axminster lie, just perfect for a pitch shot,' declared one jovial drinker. 'That may be,' declared another, 'but are you allowed to play this watering hole before the eighteenth? There should be a two pint penalty!'

Denham consulted his score card. There was nothing in the local rules to prevent his playing his next shot from inside the clubhouse, but how and to where? He strode to the bay windows overlooking the green and peered out at a sea of grinning faces. There was only one real avenue of escape – pitch through the window and the ball with any luck would clear a bank and run down towards the hole.

The voice of officialdom sensed his thoughts: 'Don't you dare smash that glass with your golf ball!' it bellowed as the occupants of the window seats moved hastily out of the firing line. Denham did not argue. Instead he slipped the casement catch, leant out for a closer study of his likely landing area, and to the onlookers' astonishment politely requested they clear a path to the pin. Sustained applause greeted his announcement that he was going to wedge the ball through the open window.

Opinion inside the bar was sharply divided. The sober faction decided he was crazy – the rest had nothing but praise for his daring. This was the spirit that had put the Great into Britain and would that there were more like him. Denham collected his pitching wedge from his bemused caddy and zeroed in on the target. At a range of twenty-five feet the rectangle of open air measured four feet by two. Respectful silence greeted his first practice swing. Several more were required before the precise weight of shot and trajectory were established.

Denham took a last deep breath – and struck his third shot to the eighteenth. The ball described a gentle parabola, neatly bisected the uprights of the window frame, and rolled down the greenside bank to pull up twelve feet below the hole. A roar of appreciation greeted Nigel as he emerged triumphantly into the sunshine.

Sadly his putt for a fairy-tale par four lingered obstinately on the lip of the cup and the final score was an unremarkable 74. But for twenty-four hours Denham was a national hero as the first man to play Championship golf from the nineteenth to the eighteenth.

Immediately afterwards the Moortown committee met in solemn session and decided that as the game was meant to be played outdoors the clubhouse and its environs would in future be out of bounds. The Rules of Golf committee of the Royal and Ancient Club of St Andrews then decreed that Denham's bogey five at the eighteenth should not have been accepted. By opening the bar window Nigel had improved his line of play. The clubhouse was an immovable obstruction and no part of it should have been moved. It was perfectly permissible for him to have changed the position of a chair or a stray shoe (as loose impediments) but opening windows was a contravention of Rule 17–1. He should have been penalized two strokes. No matter. Nigel's niche in the folklore of the game is secure, and the old adage that the best golf stories originate in the bar remains unchallenged.

Hassan Hassanein: the forgotten man

DICK SEVERINO

When Vincent Tshabalala of South Africa won the French Open at Le Touquet in 1976, his victory generated headlines, not only because he was virtually unknown outside his own country, but because he was black. Reporters on the scene could remember only one black player ever having won a national open championship in Europe, Sewsunker Sewgolum. They'd missed Hassan Hassanein.

Granted, Hassanein was an Egyptian, but Egypt is in Africa. And, with forebears from Upper Egypt, deep in the African continent, he was black – black as night without the moon. Born in Cairo in 1916, he was a marvellous golfer, with an easy flowing swing and good tempo. Good enough to win the French Open at St Cloud in 1951, twenty-five years before Tshabalala. He also won the Italian Open at Villa d'Este in 1949.

It is understandable that Hassanein was overlooked in the hectic scramble to make the deadlines at Le Touquet. Only someone who had known him or who had previous reason to research his background would have remembered that, though Egyptian, he was also black. After all, he had been dead for twenty years when Tshabalala won.

Information about Hassanein is scarce, even in Egypt, where the British introduced golf during World War I. He left no family to detail his history; and, at the once famous Gezira Sporting Club in Cairo, where he was head professional for many years, club records of his time are confined largely to tournament scores. Those records, together with information obtained from the Egyptian Golf Federation, whose records were not much more informative, and some older golf members at Gezira and the Alexandria Sporting Club, provided the following history of Hassanein.

Hassanein began golf as a barefoot caddy at the old Heliopolis sand course in Cairo. From that unlikely beginning, emerging slowly from the poverty into which he had been born, he developed into a first-class international professional, successful in tournaments in Great Britain, Continental Europe and the United States. At home in Egypt he was equally adept on grass or sand courses.

A likeable man, known affectionately to his many friends as 'Doc', with his dark skin, horn-rimmed glasses and engaging smile, when attired formally in a dark suit with a shirt and tie he resembled more a preacher from Alabama or Georgia than a golf professional from Cairo. His good nature and talent made him a splendid ambassador of goodwill for Egypt and Egyptian golf.

He won the Egyptian Open four consecutive times, 1949 through 1952, beating 1951 British Open Champion Max Faulkner, Alf Padgham, Jimmy Adams and John Jacobs of Great Britain, Norman Von Nida of Australia, Flory Van Donck of Belgium, and other famed international professionals. In those years, and through 1956, players of that calibre were attracted to Egypt and the Egyptian Open, played in the winter on grass, for two reasons: the prize money, though not exceptional, was worthwhile; and the Egyptian climate and hospitality were inviting to sun-seeking tournament professionals from colder and gloomier winter climes.

Abroad, in addition to winning the Italian and French Opens, Hassanein qualified three times for the final rounds of the British

Open. His best performance in the championship was at Carnoustie in 1953 when Ben Hogan won and he tied for seventeenth among 196 entries. He also played for Egypt in the Canada Cup tournament in 1955 at Washington, DC, and 1956 at Wentworth, and three times in George May's World Championship of Golf at Tam O'Shanter in Chicago, forerunner of today's big-money tournaments in the United States.

On the sand courses in Egypt, Hassanein won the annual Desert Open every year from 1946 through 1956, except 1955, when he was second by one stroke in that seventy-two-hole tournament played over the old sand course at the Maadi Sporting Club. Like Hassanein, the Maadi course and the Desert Open are long gone.

The man who beat Hassanein at Maadi in 1955 was Mohamed Said Moussa from Alexandria. Moussa, now forty-eight, has won the Egyptian Open nineteen times and played for Egypt in the Canada Cup and World Cup twenty-two times between 1957 and 1980, including the past twelve years. He is well known in Europe, where he plays a few tournaments each year, almost always finishing in the money.

Despite his long dominance in Egypt, however, Moussa must rank behind Hassanein. Egyptian golf and the Egyptian Open have deteriorated sadly since the hey-day of that once interesting championship, when Hassanein and then three-times British Open Champion Bobby Locke (1954) and Barnard Hunt (1956) were the winners, and a young Gary Player won the Egyptian Match Play Championship (1955). And Moussa has never won outside Egypt.

Any comparison between the two must also take into account the fact that Hassanein died suddenly at the age of forty, in 1956 or 1957 (no one in Cairo seems quite sure which year) when a kerosene stove exploded as he primed it. His tragic death deprived Egypt and the golf world of a truly great sports personality. Henry Longhurst wrote of Hassanein in the *Sunday Times*: 'His playing record must make him unchallengeably the best Oriental golfer in the game's history.' Whether Hassanein can in fact be considered 'an Oriental' is open to question; but that, coming from Longhurst, stands as a proud epitaph.

Doing a Danecki

BOB RODNEY   *Daily Mirror*

Few people make such a stain on the white radiance of eternity that their names become part of the language. And most of those achieving such distinction do so for reasons which are less than praiseworthy, like Quisling, or Boycott (not Geoffrey, of course). Indeed, sport is particularly short of examples, apart from Dr Frank Stableford, who flourishes because he promoted a most useful kind of golfing competition.

However, in the restricted circle of golf writers, we did for a brief time speak of 'doing a Danecki'. This was a somewhat elastic expression. Essentially, it implied completing a round, or rounds, in one hell of a lot. But there was a certain dream quality about it too, as if the person commissioning the act was in some respects fey, or not quite with it, or visiting from another planet, or just plain simple.

The thing arose at the 1965 Open Championship – or, rather, at the qualifying competition for it. In those days a fairly substantial field of hopefuls played two rounds on the Friday and Saturday before the big week, and some of us reporters used to drive a regular circuit between the three or four courses which were being used, trying to find something amusing to write about. I turned up at Hillside (it was either my second or third visit of the day) to discover that somebody had turned in a card of 108. As any reasonably competent club golfer might be expected to do rather better than that, it was distinctly interesting that an Open Championship competitor couldn't. Hillside in those days had a par of 70, and here we had someone playing to a handicap of 38.

It was fairly simple to discover that the perpetrator was called Walter Danecki, and that he had entered as a United States professional. But he had handed in his card some time previously.

Nobody knew him, nobody could recall what he looked like, no-one knew where he was living. Phone checks of the local hotels drew a series of blanks. A rumour that he was staying in one of the houses in the drive leading to the Hillside course started us pestering householders in defiance of journalistic codes relating to intrusion.

All of this to no avail. We gave Danecki up as a bad job – and another good story we had missed. The Royal and Ancient Golf Club of St Andrews gave him up too. So certain were they that he would never be heard of again that they arranged for a marker to accompany Danecki's playing partner, Brian Hessay, in the Saturday round.

So the R & A was just as surprised as everyone else when Danecki coolly appeared on the tee the following morning and proceeded to shoot

$$778 \quad 557 \quad 955 - 58$$
$$9610 \quad 465 \quad 546 - 55 \quad (113)$$

for a total of 221, the highest qualifying score in Open Championship history. The qualifying figure at Hillside turned out to be 151, and Walter had missed it by exactly 70 strokes.

There was, of course, no question of the bloodhounds letting Danecki do his disappearing act for the second successive day. There was also no question about who was the more embarrassed. We were.

Danecki was charming, forthright, easy to interview – and as unreal as if he had stepped straight out of the pages of *Alice in Wonderland*. He told us he was forty-three years old, he worked as a mail-sorter in Milwaukee, he had been playing golf for seven years on municipal courses where he paid one dollar fifty for a round; he had never had a lesson, and he was sure he could beat Arnold Palmer.

There was a space in the entry form where he had to write 'amateur' or 'professional' and Walter Danecki said: 'I wanted the crock of gold, so my conscience made me write down "professional". But I don't charge if I give a lesson.'

He said he had tried to join the United States Professional Golfers' Association, but had been told he must serve a five-year apprenticeship. As he had never been a member of a golf club, or a driving range, he decided he couldn't go through all that.

'What I'll do,' he announced with some firmness, 'is win one of the big ones. Then they'll have to let me in.'

Apparently Danecki was on vacation from the Post Office, and his workmates didn't know he was out of the United States. He wondered what their reaction would be when they heard he was playing in the British Open.

Our interview was tinged with a little regret. 'I was shooting good golf before I came over here,' said Danecki. 'My partner and I felt a little bit discouraged after the first day. We thought we needed two seventy-fives to qualify. But I don't like to quit. I like to play golf – that's what I came here to do.'

(Perhaps I should record that this is doing Hessay an injustice. He wasn't discouraged – he was seething.)

Nobody had the nerve to quiz Danecki on details of his round, and I don't recall anyone thick-skinned enough to ask this amazing innocent why he didn't play better. So the only explanation was: 'I have a sore right hand. Couple of years back I dug a divot and hit a tree root. It's not been right since. Once in a while it hurts, then I don't play so good. I want to say your smaller ball is right for this sort of course. If I had been playing a bigger ball I would have been all over the place.'

Well, we don't use the smaller ball in the Open any more, and you can't just declare yourself a professional and tee up in the qualifying competition. And so far as I know, only one chap has come near to achieving a Danecki since – Maurice Flitcroft, the Barrow-in-Furness crane driver who did a sort of half-Danecki when he shot 121 at Formby in the 1976 qualifying competition, but didn't start for the second round.

I think I'm right in saying the R & A gave Flitcroft's two playing partners their entry fee back, but I don't believe anyone compensated Brian Hessay. And no, I'm not sure whether a half-Nelson has anything to do with the Admiral.

It never moved after it stopped

JOHN V. MOODY   *Western Mail*

The carefree days of my youth were spent in Conwy, on the North Wales coast; and the Caernarvonshire links, a mile or so out of the town, figured prominently in our lives – my elder brother, two younger sisters and myself – first as a short-cut from home to beach, and later as a golf course.

And it is one particular stretch of those lovely, gorse-lined links which constantly comes to mind. I see it now, a still summer's day, slightly hazy, and I'm either sitting on that seat behind the eighth tee, or putting on the ninth or seventh greens. The three are within 150 yards of one another and, oddly enough, provide the only sight one has of the sea during the round.

The tide is just beginning to ebb and a flock of dunlin are busy foraging, scurrying along the edge of the water, chasing it as it recedes and then running back in as the next little wave advances, almost as though afraid to get their feet wet. Then suddenly the whole flock takes to the air, wheeling and turning, disappearing and re-appearing as the sun catches their white undersides in a display of precision flying the Red Arrows could never hope to achieve. And almost before you knew it they would be back, darting along the sand until something – a sound or sight perhaps, or just sheer exuberance – put them to flight again. And that, and the view of Deganwy just across the water with the Llandudno (Maesdu) and North Wales golf courses in the distance, is something that could never be transferred to canvas.

Having made any number of illicit dummy runs when nobody was about, I decided that there was something in this golf game after all and persuaded my father to enrol me as a junior member in the country club.

David Roberts – otherwise known as 'Dodyn' – was a member of the Artisan section of the club. He was employed as general factotum on a yacht based in the Conwy Harbour. Junior members in those days were not exactly welcome and in any case the Artisan section had the better golfers: so, I enjoyed playing with them. But the special joy of playing with Dodyn was his tendency to malapropism. During my many games with him over a period of some three years he produced enough to write a book. The first happened during our very first game together and was prompted by his young daughter, Joan, who would be about five at the time. It was an early spring morning: we had just driven off the fifth tee and she was enthralled by the sight of half a dozen lambs playing follow-my-leader, jumping off a little ledge into a grassy hollow and returning to repeat the exercise.

'What are they doing, Dad?' asked the young innocent. No immediate answer, and we began walking down the slope towards the fairway, Dodyn some thirty yards ahead of us. But he had been working on it, and suddenly he turned round with a triumphant: 'Bollocking! That's what they are doing, bollocking!'

On another occasion, we had been held up by four visitors, not a golfer among them, who had repeatedly ignored our cries of 'Fore!' until even Dodyn's patience was exhausted. On the thirteenth tee and after one final cry of 'Fore!' he let fly, drove over their heads and stumped off to give the astonished quartet a piece of his mind. 'Now look here,' he said, 'it's not just a matter of hitting the ball, you know . . . you've got to learn the adequates of the game.'

One day we were driving at the last hole and Dodyn hit one of his very best tee-shots, up and over a bank which runs across the first and last fairways, and which was normally out of his range. As was his custom when he had hit a particularly good shot he would immediately turn those faded blue eyes on me, waiting for a word of praise. 'My word, Dod, you really caught that one,' I duly obliged, which prompted him to mention for the first and only time during our friendship his limp, which I had surmised to be a result of polio.

'Not bad, considering my leg,' he said. 'Feel this.' Uncertain which one I was supposed to be testing, I clutched at the nearer one and replied: 'My word, it is thin.'

'Thin, be buggered,' he answered. 'That's the good one, feel the other.'

Arriving at his tee shot he selected his mashie niblick, a hickory-shafted relic whose blade had been so highly polished that it had long since lost any grooves it might have had. His shot flew straight at the flag, bounced once and spun back an inch or two on a green burnt brown by the sun in the height of one of those summers we seldom enjoy nowadays. This time he didn't wait for a word of praise. That familiar triumphant look on his face, he turned to me and said: 'Duw, duw John bach . . . see that? Never moved after it stopped!' There was no answer to that.

The French Ben Hogan

ANDRÉ-JEAN LAFAURIE *Golf European*

Once upon a time there was a modest French family. More exactly, the members of this family were – they still are – Basques. That means neither French nor Spanish, but it could sometimes – as in this case – mean golfer.

One day, in the evening, the family was gathered together around the table. At this time the women stood behind their husbands. No, it was not two centuries ago, but just before the Second World War, almost yesterday. But it was in the Basque country, the home of the peasants, the land workers. So there they were around the table, and the father said this:

'Boys, I have something to tell you.' He looked hard at his two sons. They were strong and dark. Like everybody in this country at this time they were not rich, but they were hard workers. The French Basque boys were either sailors or golfers – caddies, of course. Sometimes they were allowed to take a client's niblick and practise. Most of the time they did it clandestinely, at night. If they were discovered they immediately lost their jobs. No job, no money, no bread. No, it was not two centuries ago . . .

The two sons of our Basque family were caddies at St Jean-de-Luz. One day at the Chantaco Club, one day at La Nivelle, and some money to take back home every day. Life was difficult, but the two sons had the extraordinary luck of having good swings. One of them was, in fact, a really good golfer. His name was Michel. His younger brother was Jean. Weaker, a little shorter, he was also a good player, but . . .

Father, with his deep, deep voice, a colossal man, looked at him. 'Jean, you'll be a champion.'

Stupefaction! Wives stopped cooking, sons stopped eating. All looked intensely at their father. But Michel was a much better golfer than Jean! He was like a rookie professional. He was . . .

'Father, may I . . .?' Michel tried to speak, but in these times nobody spoke to the Father without permission.

Father shouted: 'I said Jean will be the champion! I've decided! From tomorrow morning he will begin practising! Eight hours a day!'

'But we have no money, Father. Not enough.'

'Michel will teach golf to the rich clients, all these British golfers who come every winter to our country. The money will keep Jean during his practising years. Later he will pay us back. When he has won the British Open.'

The British Open! Only once had a French golfer won it – again, rather, a Basque. He was born a few miles away. His name was Arnaud Massy. But times had changed. The British Open was much too hard now for a Frenchman to win.

'He'll try,' said the father, 'and he'll succeed, for sure. He will begin tomorrow morning.'

The family finished dinner in silence.

As he had said, it began the next day. Jean worked from dawn to dusk. He spoke not a word, did nothing but swing. This went on for months, during which Michel, on the other side of the course, taught rich people how not to make an air-shot every two hits.

The money Michel earned was given to the father every night:

and nobody grumbled. Jean was alone, single. 'Marriage can wait!' shouted the father. So Jean waited.

When there was enough money the father sent his son to the British Isles. There he was again a caddy, just to make a living. He played as often as possible, and he helped the head pro. He was always silent. How many words did he speak a day? Ten perhaps. 'You talk less than Ben Hogan!' the pro once told him. Ben Hogan? He had heard of him. The greatest golfer in the world, perhaps in history. To be like Ben Hogan – even if only as silent – was Jean's ambition. If only he could become as great a genius as him with a three-iron!

He never was. But once he actually met Ben Hogan. Yes, the great man came to the club to practise just before playing the British Open. (The only time, as you know, that he went to the Open. And he won.) And Jean played the practice round with him!

'I think he spoke much less than me,' said Jean. Not ten words a day, only five – if he was feeling chatty.

Now Jean is back in France. He often goes to see his father, who still lives in the Basque country. Jean is rich now. He has paid back all the money the family lent him thirty years ago. He became the greatest French golfer and, for one or two years, the best in Europe. He is still silent. He has never won the British Open, but was once leader after three rounds. No Frenchman has done better since Massy, and the father can be proud of his younger son.

That was the story – not exactly, but almost – the story of Jean Garaialde. A Basque golfer. A champion.

Wartime golf

JACK STATTER *The Sun*

This odd story of golf in occupied Europe during World War II began the day a German military car came scrunching up the gravel at Hilversum Golf Club, in Holland, watched apprehensively by the members through the clubhouse windows.

In the words of a man who was there at the time: 'We feared the worst. Out stepped a Luftwaffe officer, who knocked on the front door and asked for the secretary. He asked if it would be acceptable for him to play the occasional round of golf. The secretary was hardly in a position to refuse.

'We all watched with interest as the German went back to his car, changed into golf shoes and pulled out a bag of clubs. His chauffeur acted as caddy and off he went.

'His etiquette was impeccable. Every divot was replaced, every bunker smoothed. After his round he drove back to his fighter squadron near by. He always played on his own and never once entered the clubhouse. We got quite used to seeing him around.

'Then one black day a team of German Army engineers swarmed on the course and began to mark our mighty oak trees for felling to strengthen their "Atlantic Wall". When our Luftwaffe "country member" saw the paint marks on the trees he abandoned his round and drove off. Late in the evening the same day he returned with his chauffeur-caddy. Out of the back of their car they unloaded a number of notice boards attached to stout posts.

'These they posted at every entrance to the golf course. The secretary made it his business to be there when the German strolled back to his car, dusting his hands and wearing an air of obvious satisfaction. He grinned and said: "That should keep them off."

'The signs, which were most impressive and official-looking, read "*Achtung! Es ist verboten . . .*" and told all German military personnel that the golf course was out of bounds to them and to all German military vehicles "by order of the local Commandant of the Gestapo".

'His squadron was posted away soon after. I don't know what happened to him. Perhaps he finished up playing winter rules on the Eastern front. But when we look at these ancient trees we know that there was at least one German who had his priorities in the right order. If he called here now we would like him to come into the clubhouse. He still has many friends who remember him.'

The stuff of history

BILL CLARK *Sunday Mirror*

Nobody particularly noticed the oldest member till suddenly his stool at the corner of the bar was empty. Only a few days in hospital, we heard, and so it was. But it gave us quite a turn at the little, rather ancient club looking across the sea from County Down to the Mull of Kintyre. It was as if the Liverpool boat had ceased to emerge from Belfast Lough on the stroke of 9 p.m., or the ugly, old, out-of-tune piano had finally been banished from the premises of Helen's Bay.

Dick, of course, came shambling back, reinforced, he said, by three pints of the Royal Victoria's best blood. A slightly shrunken giant who had known all these long-gone past captains whose portraits frowned along the hall. Once again he occupied his niche on Thursday night – men only and to hell with that lib nonsense – presiding over the solemn ritual of filling in the pools coupons and collecting the stakes in a pint pot. 'We've only ever had the four aways up,' he complained as ever, 'but maybe this is the week.'

Yet his brief defection got the tongues wagging. Elderly, oft-ignored buffers found themselves being quizzed about Dick. 'Did he ever play golf? How did he earn a crust?' And back came discreet hints that the lifelong bachelor had been a bit of a lad in his day – banished to an Indian tea garden but still contriving to play to one handicap. The trouble was that nobody knew for sure. Dick was before everybody's time.

Even the council felt the need to deviate from the problems of leather-jackets, scutch grass and that business of beer chucking at the last men's dinner and realize that Dick couldn't go on for ever. 'The centenary is coming up, Mister Captain,' somebody pointed out, 'and we'll want a history of the club published. Most of it is only in Dick's head – the good stuff anyway.'

And so, being something to do with scribbling, I was delegated to interview the oracle – 'Get it down on paper just in case' was the delicate phraseology. The scheme, clumsily broached, evoked an understanding chuckle in Dick, immediate enthusiasm and an invitation to have a whisky and ask away. It was like stepping through the door of a treasury – not a museum. Dick's memories weren't the dull stuff of minute books or politicians' egotistical memoirs. They were the laughs, arguments and curiosities of eighty-odd years since he was led into the club by his father, a founding member.

There were headlines about the Polish troubles the first time we talked and Dick, gazing down the first fairway to the water, pondered – 'Dear knows what we'll do if there's another war. In the 1914–18 do we had to plough up three fairways and plant corn. What a disaster. Cost us a fortune in lost balls and nearly put some of us out of the game. We weren't having any of that in 1939. When the government talked about more corn we said we'd graze sheep instead.

'Another disaster. They broke into people's gardens and the hon. sec. had to hide from complainants. That wasn't the worst of it. Those damned animals congregated every night on the fourth green. If we put up a fence they broke it down. And they'd all pee there till morning. It killed the green for years and the putts still don't run true on it. Aye, another war would be a real headache.'

The talk of greenkeeping sent Dick's mind flicking across the decades like Doctor Who's Tardis. 'I often think about William Roseman, one of the first greenkeepers. He was cutting the third fairway on the day the *Titanic* went down the lough from Harland and Wolff's to embark on her maiden voyage. Some of us stood on the first tee watching her and feeling proud. "Come here, William, and see the *Titanic*," his wife shouted across the course. William never lifted his head. "Sure I'll see her up and down the lough plenty times," he answered, and went on cutting.

'I can see him still with the big bakery horses pulling the gang-mower. They came to Helen's Bay for their holidays, you see. After a year of walking day after day on Belfast's cobblestones their poor feet were worn right down. So the bakery gave them to us for a while. They wore thick rubber shoes not to damage the turf, did light work and went back to the roads when their hooves grew again. Far better beasts than those bloody sheep.'

Memories of the third fairway leading to the most secluded green set Dick to laughing. 'Some of us bad lads would sneak there on Sundays and putt for pennies,' he recalled. 'It scandalized the village. But eventually they allowed Sunday golf. Even a deputation of local clergy agreed it wouldn't be a mortal sin after two o'clock in the afternoon and before the bells for evening service. But we'd to give a pledge not to use caddies. That would have kept wee boys and girls out of Sunday School to make fourpence for nine holes and sevenpence for eighteen. Mind you, some of the girls needed Sunday School the way they swore at lost balls.'

The oldest member's recollection switched easily from girl caddies to lady members. 'It was the need for money that got them into the main lounge,' he remembered grimly. 'We were in debt and the captain of the day had the idea of running dances to help the funds. I voted against it because I knew we'd never get them back to their own room that used to be the farm kitchen. And I was right. We finished the season to the good but, except for Thursday nights, the ladies are in for keeps. It wasn't like that in my mother's day. She was ladies' president for donkeys years but to my certain knowledge never took a club in her hands.'

Clearly the advent of women in the big room with its elaborate bar salvaged from the burnt-out P & O liner SS *Bermuda* ended the wilder exploits. 'At least they got us home in good order,' admitted Dick. 'Not like the days when the Black and Tans operated a curfew in Ireland. We'd stay too long in the club and didn't dare set foot on a road for fear of arrest or worse. So the only way home was along the railway line. It was fine for a big fella like me. One step took me from one sleeper to the next. But some of my littler pals tumbled down the embankment from time to time and sometimes just decided to make a night of it.'

Dick believes he had his one and only golf lesson from a pro who had spent such a night. 'I'd been given five bob for my birthday,' he explained, 'and my father told me to spend it on a lesson that would set me up for life. But the pro wasn't in good form at all. He suffered agonies to stick a peg in the ground and place a ball on it. Then he told this ten-year-old child who was waiting for all mysteries to be revealed – "Draw back your club and whale into the ball like buggery." Then he departed, remembering to take the money, in search of something for a headache.'

Perhaps I'll write the history of my club some day – even the dusty bits that Dick has forgotten. And I urge you to pause a while beside the venerable gentlemen – or lady – who sits serenely in your club watching the world hack by. For those of us fascinated by the lore of this greatest of all games, they are gold mines.

Close to a miracle

PAUL MacWEENEY

There have been many stories in golfing history of amazing recoveries from apparently hopeless physical handicaps and subsequent championship triumphs – three of the most notable examples being John D. MacCormack, Ben Hogan and Jimmy Walker. Hogan, left for dead on the road after a motor smash in 1949 and sustaining multiple injuries, fought his way back to health to win three American Opens and many other tournaments. His courage was brought home to millions by the film of his life, *Follow the Sun*.

Walker, the Scottish amateur chosen for the 1959 Walker Cup team, was also involved in a car smash which cost him a knee-cap and made it improbable that he would ever walk properly again, much less play any game. He, too, gritted his teeth and positively forced himself to recover. Within a year he was back on the course and not only regained his Walker Cup place but won the Scottish championship.

In some respects, however, John D. MacCormack's experiences were, although the least publicized, the most remarkable of the three. During the first war, when serving in the RAMC, he was not only severely wounded but badly shell-shocked as well. Brought to hospital in 1916 at the age of twenty-five, his prospects even of living were regarded as slight. Live he did, but he was paralysed from the waist down and in that condition he remained for six years.

His desire to come back to the game he loved burned with an intensity as fierce as that within the minds of Hogan and Walker many years later, and in 1922 he went to London to a physician who had had outstanding successes with similar cases. Slowly, painfully but progressively, MacCormack learned to walk again. But still his hopes of actually playing golf seemed as remote as ever. And yet, within eight months of his return to Dublin, J. D. won his first championship, the Irish Close in June of 1923 – an achievement as near the miraculous as anything in the history of sport.

Wearing a steel corset lined with rubber to support muscles weakened by years of non-use, he set about regaining the power and rhythm of his swing with almost fanatical determination. He overcame intense pain and fatigue in the process, but his spirit never wavered, and never was a triumph more complete than when he beat Louis Warner, nine years his junior, in the thirty-six hole final at Milltown.

To have done that alone might have sufficed for any ordinary mortal, but the taste of success was an inspiration to J. D. and in 1924 he was ranked among the first ten amateurs in Great Britain and Ireland. He retained his Close title, beating D. E. B. Soulby in the final at Newcastle, and only just failed to bring off the double, losing to E. F. Spiller in the Irish Amateur Open at Dollymount. He won the International and National Tailteann games tournaments, and brought himself to the notice of official circles in Britain by reaching the quarter-final of the Amateur Championship at St Andrews, losing at the seventeenth to Roger Wethered.

Following triumph came bitter disappointment. His record had justified his selection on the Walker Cup team to visit the United States and duly he received his invitation. He had, by then, used up his leave, but when he applied to the Local Government

Department in which he held a position as medical inspector, for additional leave, permission was not granted. Times have changed indeed – one could not now imagine such a cold official response to the opportunity of enhancing our sporting prestige. In spite of that hard blow, J. D. was firmly established as a great player. He was, naturally, chosen for the Irish team against the English Midlands and Wales in 1924, and after a quiet period of two years, emerged again to win his third Close Championship after one of the most remarkable of all deciders in that event. Six down with ten to play against H. M. Cairnes, he won at the thirty-seventh, playing every one of those holes in par or better to score a dramatic victory.

That was his last championship success, but for a further ten years, until the age of forty-eight, he continued to catch the limelight in British as well as Irish affairs. In 1932 he finished leading amateur in the Open Championship of Ireland at Little Island in a field of all the top professionals. That same year saw the inauguration of the quadrangular internationals, and while Ireland fell heavily to England J. D. alone won his singles match, in which he beat Harry Bentley.

In 1931, he had made his finest bid to win the Amateur title, for in the semi-final at Westward Ho! he stood on the eighteenth tee all square with Eric Martin Smith, but three-putted to lose the hole and the match to the eventual champion.

He was appointed captain of the Irish team in 1934 at Porthcawl and shared in a red-letter occasion for Irish golf – the first victory over England, who were crushed by the astonishing margin of twelve to three. Ireland fell to the Scots next day, but by beating Wales took second place.

Apart from his dynamic leadership J. D. had magnificent personal success. In partnership with the youthful Joe Brown he won all three foursomes and won two and halved one of his singles, thus contributing five and a half points to Ireland's aggregate. He retained the captaincy until 1937, after which he retired full of honours from the championship and international scene.

A natural swinger of a club almost from the time he could walk, J. D. was a forceful and colourful personality. His thin, spare, wiry frame was emphasized by his unusual attire of riding breeches and a tightly buttoned jacket, with a tweed cap worn at a jaunty angle. He was a hitter of devastating power with the woods, and for a number of years was rated as the longest driver in Britain and Ireland.

It was difficult to understand how he could command such power, for he used a driver four ounces heavier and four inches longer than average, but as well as unleashing tremendous speed of club-head into the ball, he also possessed a perfect sense of timing. He was the first – but not the last – Irish player to move his right foot back on the backswing, and his all-out lash at the ball was a thrilling sight.

He was closely connected with three clubs: Portmarnock, Hermitage and Grange, and he told me that the achievement which ranked higher in his own estimation than any of his three championships was his 69 at Portmarnock in winning the Legal Cup in 1934. It was the first time that 70 had ever been broken in a medal round on the famous links, and many of the members at the time considered such a feat to be impossible.

A reserved personality who did not make friends easily and was not infrequently at odds with officialdom, MacCormack was highly regarded in his playing days by those who came to know him well; and as a match-fighter he had few equals and no superiors in the annals of Irish golf. His medical duties always came first, so he was no more than a weekend player. What he achieved was a great tribute to his skill and temperament.

Titanic Thompson, master hustler

ROSS GOODNER   *Golf Digest*

Some years ago, a tall, spare man in his early seventies came into the office and was introduced to the staff as Mr A. C. Thomas from Texas. Mr Thomas, it developed, was interested in telling his life story, for a price, of course, and the editor of the magazine had agreed to collaborate on the project. All this appeared routine enough, until it was disclosed that Mr Thomas was none other than Titanic Thompson – who, if not a notable personage in the world of sport, was legendary in the world of the sporting proposition – the greatest golf hustler of our age.

Titanic Thompson! The very name evoked memories of tales heard through the years – of an ambidextrous golfer who could shoot par either way, of a master card player who had been implicated in the murder of Arnold Rothstein, of a man so skilled of hand and eye that he could beat anybody at anything from firing pistol and rifle to shooting pool and pitching horseshoes, of a man who had made and won a million wagers in ten thousand towns over a span of more than fifty years. What's more, he was in an uncharacteristically expansive mood and agreed to demonstrate some of his skills. It was as if Merlin himself had walked in and volunteered to conduct a free seminar.

There wasn't a man present who didn't consider the next two days the most memorable and instructive of his career. First, of course, there was some scepticism, but the mood changed when, in response to a question about his legendary skill at pitching cards, Titanic dispatched someone for a new pack. Upon opening the deck, he stood at one side of the office, about twenty-five feet from a filing cabinet, and, holding each card between his first and second fingers, flipped them from a position just inches from his right ear. Working quickly and smoothly, he rifled card after card across the room, each one hitting the same spot on the cabinet. It had to be seen to be believed. In answer to the obvious question he said he had perfected the art over hundreds of hours in countless lonely hotel rooms across the land.

Next he volunteered to show us the approved method of tossing coins at a line on the floor. From a distance of about fifteen or twenty feet, Titanic lagged the coin and it stopped squarely on the line. Then, calling his shots, he made one coin hit and bounce to the right and another hit and bounce to the left. All three stopped on the line only inches apart. They could have been covered with a dollar bill or, more appropriately, with a hundred-dollar bill, which was what Titanic held in his left hand throughout the exhibition, ready in an instant to cover any foolish wager. This was legerdemain of such a high order that I, for one, reached for my wallet to make certain it was still there.

Taking up the cards again, Titanic laid out a six-card deal of Pitch, a game common to the southwestern United States. He offered to bet his onlookers that he could prevent any of us from making a bid of three with the hand he had laid out. When he got no takers, he then offered to bet he could make the bid himself. Finally, it being obvious none of us had any money to bet, he showed us how to make the bid, then demonstrated how to stop someone else. Naturally, when we tried it we failed miserably. It was uncanny.

I had seen Titanic before, years earlier, at a small golf club not far from his native Arkansas. He was standing on the putting green, idly stroking the ball – left-handed, which was his natural way – scanning the clubhouse, the car park, the home green with a practised eye. But he was known, and the club manager came out and told him to leave the premises.

Titanic Thompson had been one of the world's most talented men, and perhaps one of its loneliest, and after half a century of wandering he had a final desire to tell his life story. In due course the first couple of chapters of his book were written and put in the hands of a reputable agent, but no publisher was willing to back him. Eventually the project was abandoned. So the world missed a great opportunity; because Titanic Thompson is dead now, and I can testify that he was worth listening to.

The Doctor

LESLIE EDWARDS

There was nothing about his physique to suggest that Dr John Lawrie was a good golfer. He was heavily built, burly – incapable, it seemed, of athletic movement. He had a leonine head set deep into his shoulders. He had style, and it showed. It was almost unthinkable that he should go out without a caddy. The ball teed, he surveyed the shot from a few yards behind it and strode to his stance so imperiously and with such panache one felt he was going to hit it at least 500 yards. He did hit the ball a long way and held one year the leading gold medal at St Andrews to prove it, but his *forte* was fairway woods. No professional could have hit them more impressively.

To everyone in golf here and in the United States he was known effectively as The Doctor. He'd served on the R and A Championship Committee: had been captain at Hoylake and had several times attended the Masters tournament in Atlanta, promoted by his boyhood hero Bobby Jones. He considered Jones the finest golfer in the history of the game and the man every young golfer should try to emulate.

That he was condemned all his life to endure a stammer marked enough to daunt the bravest did not register with the Doctor. Indeed, in his worst moments of stress when he spoke publicly, it was the audience who suffered agonies of suspense while he wrestled silently (or as near silently as he could) to start a sentence. His indifference to this handicap was providential. If anything the stammer added point to what he said in that he was blessed with a lovely sense of humour.

When he came in from a match against the Oxford and Cambridge Society at Hoylake (and most of the club team that day had lost) John Graham asked him, 'Did you win?' The Doctor said he had. 'By how many?' enquired Graham. The answer after the inevitable jumble of incoherent sounds and head and stomach tilting was: 'MMM – um – er – ummm-millions.'

Yet he lacked nothing in shrewdness. Before the last round of the Open Championship at Troon in 1962 someone bet the Doctor five pounds that Palmer would not break 70. My abiding recollection of that day of melting heat is of John Lawrie marching at the head of Arnie's army of thousands of excited fans down the long sixth hole which few players were reaching with two woods, but which Palmer seemed to find the most commonplace of par fours.

When Palmer and his partner, Kel Nagle, played their second shots to the eighteenth green and Palmer was seen to be sailing serenely to an Open Championship triumph, the crowd broke ranks and stampeded on to the fairway to form a hollow square and get a closer look at the final putts. There was delay while the players and stewards struggled through massed spectators to reach the green. When order was restored Palmer, who faced a putt of several yards, sidled over to the Doctor and whispered, 'What have I got to win, Doc?' The answer, because Palmer had been told of the five-pound bet, can hardly have surprised him: 'Nnnn-um – um – nnnever mmmm-ind about www-hat you've got to ww-in. Th-th-th-um-think of mmmm-e and the www-ife and kids,' said Lawrie. 'Pppp-utt it in!'

And Palmer did.

The Doctor and Henry Longhurst in their playing days took advantage at St Andrews during an Amateur Championship of the splendid full-length driving range, now sadly part of the University precinct, which used to be run by the professional, MacAndrew. Each took two buckets of balls; each was intent on improving his driving; each bucket contained about fifty golf balls. Far from improving their driving got worse and worse. Shots flew off to all points on the horizon. It was hot work. Ultimately Longhurst completed his second bucket and rested, perspiring from his labour, while Lawrie flailed away on the adjoining tee. 'How many have you got left?' Longhurst demanded. The Doctor, red-faced, exhausted, frustrated almost

beyond words answered ruefully: 'Only tttt-en – um – more . . .
Th-ank God!'

There was another famous moment at Formby when the
Doctor, refereeing a match between Michael Bonallack and the
American Downing Gray in the Amateur Championship, was
asked at the Punchbowl green of the thirteenth: 'Whose play?'
Bonallack's ball was barely on the front edge of the green; Gray's
lay high on the bank on the left. The Doctor walked to the flag and
there made his decision. Gray was not happy about it and asked for
a measurement. This involved the Doctor in paced journeys to and
from both balls and took a considerable time.

As he walked the final few yards uphill to Gray's ball his three-
foot stride suddenly began to contract to something nearer two
feet nine inches. All this time some 200 spectators were standing in
respectful silence. There was then a moment of hiatus. The
Doctor's decision refused to come. Finally it arrived in a burst:
'Ah-um-ahb-er-solutely eee-qual!' They spun for it and Bonallack,
if my memory is correct, eventually won a fine match at the
twentieth. The gallery was still chuckling five minutes after the
Doctor's decision, but it did not bother him a bit. He'd done his
job. If there was any fun to be had from anything he had said or
done, all the better.

I am sure the Doctor would happily have used, for his own
purposes, the crack which none of us made during his lifetime and
which I make now only in the sure knowledge that he will greet it,
in the Elysian fields, with a chuckle: 'Me? I'm the original
inarticulated Lawrie!'

PART SIX

Forgive us our Press passes

There's one of 'em in there now

HENRY LONGHURST

For one as work-shy as myself I look back appalled at the amount I had cheerfully undertaken and in fact cheerfully accomplished – but really it was a marvellous life for a young man and I do honestly like to think I appreciated at the time, and not merely later, how lucky I was. For one thing newspapers are not liable to ask how old you are; all they want to know is whether you can deliver the goods. Thus you can step straight on to a rung of the ladder which a barrister, say, or even a doctor, of much greater talent might not attain till his middle thirties. I have always had a sneaking sympathy for the chap in the Bible who got the most frightful stick for thanking God that he was not as other men are, but at the risk of incurring the divine displeasure I must reveal that from this time onwards I never went to a regular place of work and even now I am either entirely at home or entirely away, probably in some far distant sunnier clime, in pleasant places among mostly pleasant people who are anyway at their pleasantest in the circumstances in which I meet them, and all this almost certainly at someone else's expense. Furthermore I have never in my life, never, worked during the afternoon. So it may be forgiven if sometimes, when I go down to see friends in the City and observe these hideous glass-box buildings and reflect that it falls to thousands of people to spend their whole working life therein, and in the same few square feet at that, I tend to feel, 'There but for the grace of God . . .' and a sort of guilty shiver comes over me in case Providence gives me the same sort of stick as the Pharisee. Still, nothing can take it away now and all one can do is to be duly thankful.

The reporting Press, as against the essayist type like Bernard Darwin, were less highly regarded then, it is fair to say, than now, but the newcomer takes it all as it comes. An evening paper requires about five telephoned reports a day to catch the various editions, to say nothing of incessant paragraphs for the Sports Diary and in the case of the *Evening Standard* the Londoner's Diary. My first assignment was an English Championship at a Yorkshire club and the accommodation for the entire Press, which, knowing no better, I did not find strange, was a small potting-shed filled with flower-pots and empty beer-bottles. On the wall hung one telephone for the lot of us. Senior members of the fraternity, notably George Greenwood, who wrote for thirty-two years for the *Daily Telegraph*, had evidently complained, and it happened that when the secretary and some official came round to investigate, I was the only person in the potting-shed. 'There you are,' I heard the secretary say. 'There's one of 'em in there now.'

The fearless prophets

MARK WILSON   *Daily Express*

It cannot have gone unnoticed, though those of us involved so often wish it could, that at the start of each Open Championship the golf writers of the popular national newspapers venture into a world more familiar to their racing colleagues. We become prophets, and make the ensuing four days of only academic interest by revealing in advance who is going to win.

Afterwards, and especially at the prize-giving ceremony when memories are still liable to be fresh, it is a subject we normally prefer not to discuss. If pressed to do so, we defend ourselves with a standard plea of mitigation. We don't do it voluntarily; our sports editors, unaware of how unreliable golfers are compared to horses, insist on the exercise.

However, seizing with grateful hands this opportunity to speak from an unaccustomed position of towering strength – yes, I got it right last year – I am now prepared to debate the issue and its many consequences. If I remember correctly, I predicted Tom Watson at Turnberry on the wild hunch that having just won four tournaments there was the slim chance that he might win another. Modesty compels me to confess to the fact that there came a stage during the final afternoon when I began thinking of my excuses for having brushed aside the prospects of Jack Nicklaus for once.

The finish of an Open usually brings me quite a number of readers' letters, most asking in the most brutal terms when I expect to get it right. This time, ironically, the postbag was much lighter, and those who did write complained that my success as golf's Peter O'Sullevan had been harmful. As one put it so succinctly: 'What you wrote in the *Express* made my bookie cut his odds, and I would be much better off if you'd got it wrong again.' Some people really know how to hurt. Little, if at all, can they appreciate the mystiques which bedevil this tipster business. There is much more to it than just stabbing the list of exempted entries with the toe of a putter. As an example, let me tell you how I – well, Bob Charles and I – won the 1963 Open at Royal Lytham. We did it with a bottle of HP sauce.

During the week of the championship, I shared a breakfast table with Bob. While I was attacking the shell of a boiled egg my concentration was suddenly broken by his 'Do you mind?' When I looked up I saw that he was handing me the sauce bottle.

'Do I mind what?' I said, because I didn't want it for spicing a three-minute egg.

'Unscrew the cap for me, please,' Bob answered. 'It's a little tight.' If you get the chance some time, have a close look at Bob's hands. After pounding golf balls all over the world they are strong enough to bend iron bars, let alone open sauce bottles. So I displayed my frail fingers which ache from just using a typewriter and hit back hard:

'Give me a brush and I'll do your shoes, too.' Then he explained that it was a serious and genuine plea. Before playing an important round he preferred not to risk straining his hands for fear that it might ruin his putting touch. Suitably humbled and impressed, I obliged, and how we went on to win the Open is history. It taught me an important lesson, and one that has troubled me ever since.

Suppose I think Nicklaus is going to win at St Andrews. Before committing my hunch to print should I confront him in the Royal and Ancient Clubhouse and ask: 'Jack, are you by any chance jeopardizing your putting by opening sauce bottles at breakfast?' I know what would happen – his look would burn me into the wall like a blast of radiation. So I gamble and tip him without knowing.

Forecasting the winner of the Derby, no matter what O'Sullevan may say, is a pushover compared with the Open. Mainly, I believe from experience, because horses can't talk and golfers can, and do. The golf writer enjoys many privileges in his life and none is more envied by the ordinary fan, I guess, than our locker-room access to the superstars. It is a two-edged sword at prophesying time.

Any preconceived notions I may have on walking through the door this year will be shattered immediately on talking to Gary Player, whose powers for positive thinking make Norman Vincent Peale sound like the world's worst pessimist. One minute with him is enough to convince me that he cannot conceivably lose. Then there will be Tom Watson expounding why Jack Nicklaus is the greatest and must always be the favourite. So I'll change my mind and decide to go with The Bear – until Lee Trevino bounces in off the course. He says things like he's not quite sharp and maybe we ought not to take too much notice of the 27 to the turn he's just shot. That's when I shut my notebook, make an urgent telephone call to my sports editor, and plead: 'Must I?'

To have any chance of being a successful tipster it is vitally important to understand the temperaments of these superstars. It has always been so, right back to the 1876 Open at St Andrews when Davie Strath tied for victory with Bob Martin and then in a fit of pique refused to play off for the title. It seems that he had already endured his fill of aggravation. On the Long Hole, playing the final round of the championship alongside casual green-fee hackers exerting their public links rights, Davie hooked a drive and considered himself unfairly punished by the direction the ball took after striking Mr Hutton, a local upholsterer, on the forehead.

After finishing, to tie, Davie had a complaint lodged against him – not by Mr Hutton, but by another player whom he had also hit on the way round. While volunteers were being sought to form a committee to sit in judgement, Davie's patience ran out. He told Martin he could have the title and left.

The riches and adulation involved in victory today make such a cavalier attitude impossible. But they still have their funny ways. Nicklaus has an involved ritual for putting on his shoes and socks. It all has to be done in a set sequence. Then there's his lucky penny for marking the ball on the greens. Hubert Green must wear his faded blue shirt. They all have a favourite numbered ball. If you were to unzip their golf bags and tip them out there would be an avalanche of rabbits' paws, four-leaf clovers, stones with holes in, and other miscellaneous good-luck symbols.

Some, particularly John Schlee, believe their chances of success are directly linked to the position of the moon and stars. Don't laugh, please – I made the mistake of thinking John was having me on when he said his astrological chart was in a favourable 'go situation' for the 1973 US Open at Oakmont. It took a record closing 63 from Johnny Miller to prevent him winning. And is that any more strange than Billy Casper feasting on buffalo steaks to make up seven shots in nine holes on Arnold Palmer for another US title?

I trust now, just as we steel ourselves to go over the top once more as fearless prophets, that I have said enough to prove that it is a most unenviable task. So much can go wrong for so many things are beyond our control. My tip might well go into the final round this week with a ten-shot lead. But I would still worry. He could always get at the HP sauce bottle while I'm not looking and wreck our chances.

Fuzzy says I should stick to dominoes

RENTON LAIDLAW   *The Standard*

You might be fooled into believing that every golf writer would benefit from the careful study of the superstars on whom he reports. This is not always the case. I, for example, have a figure which is similar to Lee Trevino's but I often play like Laura Baugh. (That is unfair, I am doing Laura an injustice. Bernard Gallacher, a close friend, once cruelly commented that were I to hit my weight I would average a 400-yard drive.)

Somehow, my co-ordination is not always perfect and it can fall apart completely in serious competition. Like the time I played with American Jerry Heard at La Manga, in Spain. I played with Jerry when he was still an aspiring superstar, before his awful slump. (I plead not guilty to being an accessory. Honestly, I had nothing to do with his demise even though the evidence against me is overwhelming.)

Peter Townsend had warned him. I was the fellow who in partnership with Peter had not counted once in an earlier round. Angel Gallardo, the smiling Spaniard, had alerted him to look away when I was driving for fear of contamination and Brian Barnes, unsympathetically, had told him about my 'fresh air' shot on the first tee at Sotogrande which had even the local resident millionaires chortling. I felt that was an intrusion into private grief.

Jerry was pleasant, tolerant, even humorous for eight holes and then he cracked. Politely, but through clenched teeth, he asked to examine my clubs. He grabbed a six-iron from my tatty bag and shook his head in disbelief. He waggled the four-iron around to convince himself that the head was not really loose. He hardly had the pitching wedge out of the bag but it was thrown back in. Weighing each word carefully, he announced: 'This is easily the worst set of clubs I have ever seen in my life.' I winced . . . the man from whom I had borrowed them was standing (red-faced) just two yards away and appeared to be on the brink of a fit.

The interrogation continued: 'What ball are you using?' I cringed. I had lost all my new balls in practice and forgotten to purchase a fresh supply. I'd had to resort to digging out balls from the pockets of my friend's bag. I murmured the name of a make not recognized by the R and A, the USGA, or indeed anyone.

'Give the ball to me!' he ordered. I threw him the battered, bruised and badly discoloured ball, which he promptly hit into the thickest rough. 'That gets rid of that!' he said, rubbing his hands, well satisfied. Personally, I was surprised how well the ball had flown despite the deep cut I had inflicted in the cover two holes earlier.

An hour or so later – it seemed like weeks – the game was nearly over. Driven on by fear I had hit the last green in three shots and was putting for a par four net birdie three with the ball Jerry had given me – he had a forgiving streak. Quietly he approached me.

'Remember I carry forward the team score, not my own,' he whispered. 'This putt could mean a lot of money to me.'

'Leave it to me,' I said, bravado welling up inside. But then I pointed out that now I was really under pressure.

'I know, I know,' he said quietly, then filling his lungs full of air he shouted at the top of his voice: 'You can't putt any worse than you did when there was no pressure!' Frankly I thought that tremendously rude, so I comfortably missed the putt. Even we high handicappers have some pride.

That was a long time ago. I have improved since then, thanks to the combined help of John Jacobs, Bernard Gallacher, Brian Barnes, Tommy Horton, Clive Clark, Peter Alliss, Nick Job, Tony Jacklin, Brian Waites . . . the list is endless. Of course, it was in their own interest to help me improve. They knew I was going to be around for some time. Professionals no longer turn away on the tee these days for fear of ruining their own swings by association. They have steeled themselves to watch. Indeed my reputation as a player has been restored, renovated and refurbished.

So much so that when Arnold Palmer was playing Phoenix and putting poorly he spotted me in the crowd and came across for some words of consolation and advice . . . well, he came across to speak anyway. Fuzzy Zoeller went into paroxysms of laughter when I described my swing problems and wandered off muttering that I should take up dominoes. Gary Player, on the other hand, listened intently to my plea for advice, nodded wisely, then replied by telling me about one of his greatest rounds. I never could understand why. Maybe he had misunderstood my question.

Keeping tabs on the pros

RON MOSELEY   *Press Association*

For more than ten years Alex Sanderson and his wife June have lived a nomadic existence, travelling the length and breadth of the British Isles to provide golfing spectators, officials, players and Press with instant scores from the course. They are official scorers to the European Tournament Players Division.

It is a complex system, and occasionally it goes wrong. The Sandersons employ a lot of casual labour, mostly students, to take returns from players, relay them back to base and put figures on the scoreboards. Once unwittingly they took on a dyslexic, and assigned him to work on a leader board. Several hours elapsed before it was drawn to their attention that 'Brown' was coming out as 'Zvagt'.

A lot of things seem to go wrong in Ireland. One Irish casual scorer didn't even know what a green looked like. He had been told to go to the seventeenth, was given precise directions how to get there, and eventually found his way to the tee clearly indicated by the numbered box. Getting from that spot to the green proved a more difficult task. One man was told that the scorers should be inconspicuous. He hid himself so well that the players couldn't find him. Eventually, Alex had to go out and search the bushes for him.

The co-operation of the players is vital and most of them willingly play their part. But one or two temperamental stars do not like their concentration being disturbed and sometimes refuse to give their figures, or hand in fictitious ones. Then the system goes haywire.

Said Alex: 'It's almost invariably the same players. One or two are even rude to the scorers, but they're only doing a job, just like the players themselves. The stupid thing about this is that competitors are usually as interested in the scores of other players as the spectators. Watch the board at the end of the second day when those players on the borderline are anxiously working out what score is going to make the cut.'

Alex, who worked in shoemaking and engineering firms and was with the Army in Korea, had his own garage when he accidentally fell into the golf scoring business. He was at Stand Golf Club, Manchester, where he is a keen single-figure amateur, when a vacancy cropped up in the *Daily Express* scoring team. He became a regular and was asked to take control of the operation when the newspaper eventually withdrew its sponsorship.

At first all he had was a simple free-standing scoreboard, with the staff accommodated in caravans. Then he decided to convert a fifty-foot articulated lorry, using the side for the scoreboard and adapting the interior into working and living areas. The lorry is divided into four sections, including two bedrooms that can be partitioned off, with six bunk beds, kitchen with cooker and washing facilities, as well as conveniences such as television, radio and bar.

From May to October the Sandersons are rarely at their home in West Haughton, Lancashire for more than a few days at a time. They have been known to finish one job in Scotland on a Sunday evening and then travel 400 miles through the night, getting set up ready for another tournament in the London area by eight o'clock the following morning.

They have had many harrowing experiences trying to find their way with their massive lorry through narrow country lanes to obscure courses. On one occasion map-reader June directed them along a narrow road only to come across a low bridge that could have taken the top off the vehicle. Backing the monster about a mile in pitch dark was an experience they don't want to repeat.

Three other members of the Sanderson family help out – daughter Daryl and son Mark occasionally, and son Alan permanently. Alan, BA in Economics, is the mathematical genius. He masterminds the operation at base, watching out for obvious errors and instantly converting scores into plus and minus par and relaying them to all parts of the course.

June directs operations in the Press tent where, for most of the bigger tournaments, there is a separate scoreboard; while Alex keeps himself in reserve as a trouble-shooter. He does intensive planning throughout the winter months, formulates new ideas and renovates all the equipment.

'If I've done my job properly then there should be nothing for me to do during a tournament,' said Alex. 'It's only when things go wrong, or someone needs a break, that I get into the act.'

The Sandersons work long hours. Their day starts at 7.30 a.m. when the first players tee off, and sometimes does not finish until nine or ten at night when they are stripping the scoreboards and preparing them again for the following day. Alex expects that the scoring will one day be computerized, but his experience of such systems makes him wary. 'Our present method is as fast and accurate as any I have ever seen.'

Darwin's other sport

FRANK BUTLER   *News of the World*

As a sports editor I have always considered that sports writing gives trememdous scope to those with a flair for juggling words. In America, for instance, successful writers like Damon Runyon, Paul Gallico and Quentin Reynolds, the latter becoming even more famous later as a broadcaster, emerged from newspaper sports pages. Bernard Shaw wrote at length on important fights of the twenties and produced thousands of well-chosen words for the *Observer* on the Jack Dempsey-Georges Carpentier epic of 1921, which produced the first ever million-dollar gate for any sport.

Today some of the best writing is still done by sports writers, none better than by those who follow golf.

Like many of my generation, I was a devoted reader of Bernard Darwin. Surprisingly, this superb writer first won me over in my teens on the subject of boxing. Being the son of an enthusiastic boxing writer, I was brainwashed into reading all the epics of the old prize ring, followed by the great fights of Sullivan, Corbett, Fitzsimmons, Jeffries and Johnson. While I was still at school, birthday presents were usually books such as Bernard Shaw's *Cassel Byron's Profession*, and Conan Doyle's *Rodney Stone*.

One such gift was a book by Bernard Darwin, *John Gully and His Times*. It was beautifully written. Gully was a prize-fighter from Bristol. But he was much more than this. Apart from becoming champion of England, he worked as a butcher, spent time in the King's Bench Open Prison for debts, became a publican, professional backer, bookmaker, twice winning owner of the Derby, owner of coal mines, and a Liberal MP for Pontefract. Darwin's skill was such that he made Gully's antics just as fascinating as the historic victory of Bobby Jones over Cyril Tolley in the British Amateur of 1930 at St Andrews.

When I joined the *Daily Express* as a junior in the mid-thirties I was still a Darwin fan and hoped one day to be privileged to be allowed to write on golf. The golf writer of the *Express* at this time was Leo Munro. I felt honoured to go about with him and be allowed to telephone his copy, written meticulously in neat handwriting. There wasn't the same pressure to catch early editions in those days. With Munro I met the young Bobby Locke on his first visit from South Africa. I also met Henry Cotton, who was to become so helpful when I eventually got on to the courses as a reporter.

I learned a lesson the hard way on my first visit to St Andrews in 1946. With youthful enthusiasm I followed the leaders. I hadn't realized those first nine holes on the Old Course took the inexperienced way, way from the essential tool of the reporter – the telephone. I was torn between enthusiasm and dedication to see every stroke before getting to the phone in time to catch the first edition. Obviously, the best story in the world is bad news if it misses the edition.

But I hung on till the last possible minute before breaking away from Locke. I started walking back fairly quickly, but I had miscalculated the distance. Soon I was trotting and finally sprinting before breathlessly reaching the phone.

Television has changed the methods of reporting in all sport. Even the most accomplished descriptive writer has problems competing with picturesque scenes, huge crowds and controversial incidents when millions are sitting at home watching the events on colour television. They have seen the outstanding shots or freak and controversial incidents played back several times. But this is the essential challenge to the writer.

Golf before the tented village

GEOFFREY COUSINS

Being old enough to remember reporting and golf-watching conditions sixty years ago, I never cease to marvel at the facilities for communications enjoyed by the present generation. But some of my senior colleagues can also recall the days when scarcely any arrangements for informing Press and Public existed. Even at some big championships the only source of information was often just a small board near the clubhouse on which an official, using the printed draw-sheet (if one existed) would write the scores or results of matches.

Caddies wore no numbered arm-bands, nor named jackets, and no interim scores were sent in to headquarters by walkie-talkies. Journalists, of course, had their own means of keeping track of progress, being better able to identify players and pooling their information as they followed individual matches. But the uninitiated spectator was often completely in the dark as to who was playing, how they were scoring, and what happened to them in the end. Even seasoned reporters in events like the Amateur Championship would have to waylay players returning from distant parts of the course to extract the results. If neither player was instantly identified there had to be a protracted and embarrassing cross-examination. Fortunately most caddy-bags in those days bore the owners' initials, and a hurried reference to the draw-sheet would usually supply a clue.

Some of the arrangements, even at the most important championships, were frightfully inadequate and, since they were in the hands of the host clubs to a large extent, there were great differences in the quality of the 'service'. Even the R and A Championship Committee, or rather the Chairman and Secretary, who ran the show in double harness, were cavalier in their treatment of spectators. Of course, 'The Press' was scarcely considered at all.

When the Open was at St Andrews the draw for the next day was posted at the end of play, not in a prominent position where the public could read it, but in the window at the tradesmen's entrance of the R and A clubhouse. Journalists and caddies were aware of that fact and a mixed crowd of writers and carriers assembled in front of the slip of paper when it appeared.

The caddies were lucky. One had only to note the time of one's employer and buzz off to his hotel with the information. The writers, or those who had to give the full draw for publication next day – that was a regular practice in those days – had to copy out all the times as best they could, often in fading light. The draw was important because all the names went into the hat and the leader might come out first, last, or at any point in between.

Since little co-operation could be expected from the promoters, journalists had to organize their own information services. In the case of agency representatives the usual practice was to engage unemployed caddies as messengers to carry reports from the course to the base, which was usually a telephone installed by the Post Office placed in a public call-box behind the Press tent. But in 1938, when the Walker Cup match was decided at St Andrews, the Press Association used a field telegraph system with the help of the local military, mobilized by Colonel Andrew Brown. One point was at the 'loop', another behind the wall at the fourteenth, and another behind the road at the seventeenth. With the aid of runners, the reporter with each match could provide almost a hole-by-hole running story, which was received in the 'Operations Room' on the third floor of the Grand Hotel, and relayed to London on a normal PO line.

This was all very nice and neat for the PA boys, but the newspaper writers had to go out on the course to get their copy, and spend most of the day there, going from match to match, exchanging information, and gradually putting together the story.

The field telegraph system was a step in the right direction and after the war, also at St Andrews, the first walkie-talkies made their appearance. But progress was still slow and, apart from communications, the facilities for spectators had not changed very much from the early days, when a beer-and-sandwiches tent and primitive toilet facilities, consisting largely of flapping hessian screens, were considered adequate.

It was not until 1962 that the famous 'tented village' was erected at Dalmahoy for the Senior Service tournament, and this was a real breakthrough. Under stretches of gleaming white canvas were housed bars, restaurants, closed circuit TV sets, hot and cold running water and flush toilets, plus tubular steel stands and a complete information service from the course. It had never been done before on that scale, but from then on no self-respecting promoter could do anything but follow suit.

The Press – friends or foes?

KEN SCHOFIELD *Secretary, European Tournament Players Division, PGA*

I was very happy and interested to receive a letter outlining the Association of Golf Writers' plan to compile a bedside book of golf. But wait – this was not just a circular to Hon. Member Schofield. There was a PS. Obviously their idea of the fast-ball: you know, Denness and Fletcher facing Lillee and Thomo before the issue of steel headgear. 'Schofield's subject – The Golf Press – friends or enemies?' Get out of that, little man, I could hear them saying. He's got no chance.

Right, I thought, that does it. Friends or enemies? The sods. Play them at their own game, I will. They'll never find out my inner feelings. A gentle discourse on ETPD playing eligibility; format of play; and appearance money. That'll show them who KDS is and what he stands for.

But you and I know that these are subjects the Press never even touch upon. Their main interest lies in qualifying for places in sponsors' pro-ams, checking out touring pros' latest tips on technique in order to be successful in such pro-ams, and nipping in and out of the Coral betting tent to capitalize on all victories.

Damn it, one Press chap hit a full seven-iron stone dead at the final hole to stop me gaining a point for the Scots in the annual challenge with the 'auld enemy' at Royal Mid-Surrey. How much writing can he do if he's that good on the course? They're all the same.

Michael Williams keeps moaning that slow play has become the game's greatest disease. For goodness' sake, can't they all see that it's essential for our three-ball matches to take five hours so that we don't have to recruit more eight-handicap pros to fill tournament fields? We can't charge the public £5 or more to come along and not see any golf before 6 a.m.

Friends or enemies? It must be obvious already that I'm completely neutral . . . possibly erring slightly on the side of friendship. Can't have that. Think of the Tournament Committee's reaction. Right, this chap Wilson – *Daily Mail*, I think – takes a bit of a liberty ringing up Neil Coles all the time for inside information. He'll do anything to be one up on the Beaverbrook correspondent, Michael McDonnell.

Perhaps Max Faulkner's line on two great contemporary teachers of the game will sum up my real view of the scribes. Said Max: 'Well, of course they are nice chaps, but they should all be locked up.'

So you want to be Press Officer at the Open?

GEORGE SIMMS

You park the car in the garage, having driven the last fifty miles home by sheer instinct. On weary legs you drag the luggage from the boot, and head for the door.

'Had a good time then?' says The Man Next Door, one foot on the garden fork.

'Tiring, y'know.'

'Not a golf lover myself, game's too slow, but saw a bit on the box of that fellow who won – Will Rodgers.'

'Bill Rogers.'

'Aye. Envy you, though. Always fancied the newspaper game myself. Better than sitting in an office eight hours a day, five days a week.'

The grass, of course, is always greener on the other side of the garden wall. When the escape through the front door is finally made there is time to put up the tired feet, pour a large one and reminisce on how things have changed since one first became sheepdog to the world's Press back in 1964. One reflects that in 1964 the Press marquee was eighty feet by forty feet and sited on a spare bit of greensward at the back of the eighteenth at St Andrews. It has long since made way for Reserved Stand accommodation at subsequent Opens.

Until that year, 'accreditation of the Press' at the Open consisted of the Secretary of the R and A giving the Secretary of the Association of Golf Writers handfuls of Press passes, which the AGW Secretary dished out to those who turned up, in between doing his own stories for the four or five editions of his London evening newspaper. One wonders how he would have coped with today's 500 golf reporters, news and feature writers, sob sisters, photographers, messengers, radio teams, and wire-photo crews from some twenty countries, whose working conditions are the responsibility of the Press Officer.

From that eighty-foot marquee of 1964 has mushroomed a canvas Big Top of which Bertram Mills would have been proud. Around 225 feet by 75 feet it houses a 'working Press' area capable of seating 200 at a time; a hole-by-hole scoreboard fifty feet long and ten feet deep posting the scores 'as they happen' of all 150 players; a closed-circuit television area; a cafeteria; and an interview theatre – where the real dramas unfold.

It is in this interview room that the famous and the not-so-famous reveal where they thought they went right or where they thought they went wrong – a four-day saga of birdies, eagles, bogeys, elation and despair. And within moments of the story being told the telephone lines, telex links and air waves are spreading the word abroad. One reflects over a second large one that in 1964 there was a blackboard and chalk on which the ninth hole and leading scores were written and a wet rag to rub them out again.

By comparison, the Open Championship reporter of today need only find his way to the Press Centre, take his prescribed seat in front of the hole-by-hole scoreboard and, in effect, say, 'Fetch me Jack Nicklaus'. He need never leave the Press Centre in order to do his job. He need never go to the first tee or the eighteenth green, and there are cynics among us who say that some never do.

Being granted Press facilities to cover the Open is not dissimilar to getting eight draws in a row on the Treble Chance. Your Sports Editor applies in advance on the proper form – not when the Secretary of the Association of Golf Writers is doing his midday edition piece on the opening day.

Other non-starters include:

'I write a golf column for the Shepton Mallet *Clarion*.'

'We have five amateurs from our area among the 1000 who have entered for the Championship, and want to cover their attempts to qualify.'

'We would like two Press passes and two car park labels and would you please address them to me c/o Room so-and-so.'

'I am writing a book on the golf swing.'

'I would like to include a report in our College magazine.'

'I would like to take some pictures and see if I can sell them to the golf magazines.' Inevitably a few slip through the net. One remembers in the early days two immaculately attired gentlemen, shooting sticks and binoculars to boot, who declared that they worked for a regional TV company and had come to do 'voice over' reports each night. I bought it for a while, and often wonder where they are now.

But it was all part of being the whipping boy of the world's Press for two decades. By way of compensation, one has been at the centre of things.

Tony Lema in 1964 dispensing champagne in the Press tent at St Andrews for a victory that resulted from only one hurried practice round; Jack Nicklaus winning the first of his three, at Muirfield, in 1966; Roberto de Vicenzo, who 'only came to see his friends', triumphing at last at Hoylake; the emotions of Tony Jacklin's Open in 1969 – eighteen years after a Briton last did it; Doug Sanders's historic missed three-footer at St Andrews; Trevino's successful defence of his title at Muirfield in 1972 which wrecked Nicklaus's bid for the third leg of the Grand Slam that year; Tom Weiskopf wishing his father had lived just three months longer to savour his triumph at Troon in 1973; Gary Player's third at Lytham in 1974; and Tom Watson's thirty-six hole shoot-out with Nicklaus at Turnberry in 1977.

A couple of large ones, and an hour reminiscing with the feet up, does wonders for the revival processess, and one finds the energy for a stroll around the garden.

He's still there – The Man Next Door.

'That's you finished, then?'

'Just until September.'

'What's happening then?'

'The Ryder Cup at Walton Heath. Europe versus America, you know.'

'Press Officer again?'
'Right.'
'Can't be bad, can it?'
'Well, it's better than starving.'

Abandon Press tent!

STAN LINCOLN

A golf writer's job can be a hazardous one. In the days when there were no scoreboards, radio links, nor computers, competition between news agencies and newspapers was far greater than today.

I recall covering the Open Championship at Royal Lytham and St Annes in 1963 when Bob Charles, the left-handed New Zealander, beat the American Phil Rodgers by eight strokes in a play-off over thirty-six holes. I was on the course with the late Graham Emery for the Press Association. Time was vital.

To save time and the long walk back from the ninth hole, at the far end of the course, we used to climb over the spiked iron railing and telephone some of our evening paper copy to London from a call box at the next turning.

It was Emery's turn to 'flash' the ninth hole position in the second round and, as he climbed over the railings, one of his trouser legs caught in a spike. He ripped his trousers as he fell and put his arms out to try to save himself. He landed on his hands and knees and broke both wrists.

When he returned to London he claimed a new pair of trousers on expenses. After explaining how the accident happened to the powers that be he was told: 'We will allow you a new pair of trousers on this occasion, but don't let it happen again!'

On a couple of occasions I have been lucky not to be seriously injured or killed. While I was reporting the Dunlop Masters Tournament at Portmarnock in 1965 a violent gale and ferocious rain blew the Press tent down as we were telephoning our midday copy to London. All the telephone cables were ripped out and all lines were dead. Play was abandoned for the day, and John Baker from the *Exchange Telegraph* took a taxi back to our hotel in Dublin, only to find that there was a long delay on calls to London.

Through the good offices of the Independent Newspapers they sent a message over their private wire to PA sports telling them to telephone me. PA got in touch with Extel and we were able to finish our reports without too much delay.

Then there was the occasion at Hoylake during the 1975 amateur championship when the cross beam of the marquee snapped in two. All day a gale force wind buffeted the tent, and it finally caved in at 8 p.m., narrowly missing four colleagues and myself. The telephones were put out of order, but the Royal and Ancient did an excellent job getting a new marquee erected ready for the following morning.

Accuracy and speed were the hallmarks of the PA; and this got Emery and me into a scrape at the 1947 Open Championship at Hoylake. Leaders were not out last in those days: two rounds were played on the last day. When Daly finished his fourth round in 72 he was cheered and carried shoulder high off the last green.

By mid-afternoon we had sent the message 'Daly won' around the world; Daly was celebrating in the clubhouse; and the local paper, hailing the Ulsterman as the winner, was selling on the streets of Liverpool. Then the American amateur, Frank Stranahan, came to the eighteenth hole requiring a two to tie.

We held our breath as Stranahan played the almost perfect shot from 150 yards. The ball pitched on the green and ran on and on, peeped into the hole and thankfully stayed out. What a sigh of relief we gave as Daly became the first Irishman to win the coveted championship.

PART SEVEN

Golf over foreign fields

The European Tour

MARK WILSON *Daily Express*

They got it all wrong when they took away my Army war correspondent's uniform and posted me to the European Tour as a golf writer. If they had really wanted me to relax, then it should have been the other way about. I've known a few battlefronts less demanding than living with 300 tournament professionals crusading through fourteen countries each season. However, the frenzied years I have spent jet-hopping anywhere and everywhere from St Andrews to Sardinia now reward me with a storehouse of great believe-it-or-not memories, and just a few regrets:

I was there, thankfully, when the locker-room attendant at the German Open took it upon himself to disqualify an amazed British player for dusting his shoes with a club towel. But I don't suppose I'll ever forgive myself for missing the sight of burly Ryder Cup star Brian Barnes playing one-handed hockey with his putter during a particularly frustrating French Open at St Cloud, and failing to hole out even after some fifteen attempts.

At the time I was in another corner of the course, engrossed in watching an Italian professional whose suffering had taken him to breaking point. Suddenly, on missing from inside a yard he threw first his ball, then his club and finally himself over an out-of-bounds fence into a wheatfield. He disappeared, never to be seen again, with an anguished scream that would have done justice to any kamikaze pilot.

The unique structure and cosmopolitan appeal of the European Tour promotes, and, indeed, thrives upon such strange happenings, while at the same time fostering through the incentive of £2,000,000 in prize money a continually improving standard of play. Severiano Ballesteros, the handsome, dashing young Spaniard, is the most impressive evidence to be offered in support of this fact.

One statistic is sufficient to justify the claim to uniqueness: the April-through-October tour brings into competition each week the best players of nineteen nations, ranging from hardened globetrotters to rookies who can get lost looking for the showers in the Wentworth clubhouse. Certainly no other golf circuit in the world boasts such an international image or demands more skills for the mastering of every possible permutation of course and weather. One week it can be a parkland challenge in the Mediterranean sunshine, the next a Scottish links in a howling gale. It is a way of life that can send an American superstar home after the briefest of visits complaining that it will take him a month to find his true swing again.

The first five weeks of the Tour are always tough, especially with the Portuguese, Spanish, Italian and French championships leading to a rapidly changing diet of sardines, paella, pasta and (I don't lie) snails. Believe me, golf talent alone is not enough to guarantee success: you need a cast-iron constitution as well. When players say, as they frequently do, that their chances of winning vanished in the men's room, no explanation is needed.

Expense too comes high on the worry list: only the top fifteen in a Continental tournament can expect to make a profit.

The Portuguese Open, traditionally the launching point for each new season, was often staged at Penina in the Algarve. Henry Cotton built the monster course from a rice field and not a few tortured pros have wished he hadn't. But those who do manage to play well on this demanding course walk on air and develop a healthy appetite, even for sardines.

The Spanish Open which follows has yielded some fascinating

moments. One year at La Manga we had Arnold Palmer coming to the last hole needing a birdie to tie, and then powering an eagle three for victory. On another occasion in Spain I saw a thoroughly bemused challenger drop to his knees and hole out by using his putter as a billiards cue. He would have carried on playing too, had not his Australian partner bunched a huge fist under his nose and pointed to the clubhouse with the other hand.

It is the Italian Open that provokes the wildest events, however. I am grateful for Providence having placed me beside the green when Brian Barnes, once again, met the stubborn spectator. On the way to a shared victory and then a play-off defeat, Brian politely asked the spectator, the only one in sight that day at Monticello, to move away from the line of his birdie putt. There was a firm shaking of the head, an exchange of words in English and Italian, a violent waving of arms, and eventually the calling of a policeman who demanded to be told the facts of the affair in minute detail.

With the air of a Supreme Court judge, the policeman found for the spectator – he had paid his money and was entitled to stand where he wanted. But in fairness to Barnes, the spectator was ready for a compromise. He would stand still and let Brian move his ball to another part of the green so that he wasn't on the line. The logic of it appealed to the policeman, if not the Rules of Golf. So Barnes got down to work, holed the putt, and left the spectator wondering what all the fuss had been about. More unfortunate was the Italian player who three-putted. This so infuriated one of his supporters that he rushed across and punched him on the nose.

It was at the Italian Open in 1978 that the young Ryder Cup player, Mark James, decided to play his second round with one hand. He shot 111 on the Pevero course – a Robert Trent Jones creation – in Sardinia, saying he would have broken a hundred but for having to play round the edge of every lake. The point was that James was protesting, in his own strange way, against a shortage of caddies.

This shortage is a frequent problem on the Continent, and women are often employed as caddies. Some are enormous, muscular mothers, others beautiful, slender and distracting belles.

Which reminds me of a Swiss Open and a professional who shall be nameless and treated with compassion, because five weeks away from home can test the fortitude of any man. He engaged the most attractive of all the lady caddies for his opening round, and, possibly because he failed to keep his mind completely on golf, made a disastrous score. Both player and caddy took it badly. He swore and she cried. Later that warm, sunny afternoon, another player was searching for his ball in the long grass when he tripped over the pair of them. They were, they said, consoling one another.

Another year at Crans-sur-Sierre there was the classic case of The Nude Golfer at the Bar. When called before PGA officials for trial, the offender pleaded not guilty on the grounds that he was not technically naked when standing at the bar in the village pub drinking his beer. He had, and there were scores of witnesses, male and female, to prove it, rolled his underpants into a ball and placed them on his head. When one of the ladies present, the wife of a player, was asked her reaction to the incident she calmly stated that she hadn't been all that impressed with what she saw. This condemnation was said to have hurt the defendant a lot more than the official PGA punishment which followed.

The glory of Augusta

JOHN FENTON *British Broadcasting Corporation*

When the opportunity came for me to broadcast from the US Masters Tournament at the Augusta National Golf Club in the State of Georgia I knew that it was going to be unlike anything I had seen in several years of watching tournaments in Britain.

The magic starts when the car turns off the highway into Magnolia Lane, the straight quarter-mile approach to the clubhouse. Many a famous player has felt his insides turning to water as he approaches this Mecca for the first time.

It all began back in 1934, when the late Bobby Jones had the idea of inviting a few professionals along to Augusta to play in a tournament. He was initiating an event which would grow to be the most prestigious tournament in the world, an event which would fill the greatest players with apprehension and longing. Trevor Homer, the English amateur, captured the competitors' feelings when he referred to Augusta as the 'ultimate laxative'.

The famous Augusta azaleas had already bloomed and faded by the time of my visit, and so the dominant colours were green and white. The clubhouse, locker room and professional's shop, adjoining one another and built on a gentle slope, provided the long splash of white. The green was supplied by the beautiful lush fairways which meander up and down through woods of long-needled pine trees. Further splashes of white appeared where the fiendishly-positioned bunkers ate into the fairways or isolated the undulating greens. Although there are fewer than thirty of them, these silvery traps are large and ever-threatening, and none of them is there as an ornament.

Before visiting the US Masters I had a mental picture of American golf spectators as a Coke-swilling, hot-dog-chewing bunch of loud-mouthed Yankees. This illusion was quickly dispelled at Augusta. The green-painted refreshment stalls out on the course merge quietly with the pinewoods. And the prestige of the US Masters seems to put everyone on their best behaviour. Tickets are hard to come by and strictly limited. There's no 'pay at the gate', so unless you have obtained a ticket in advance, there is absolutely no point in turning up.

There is an added incentive for the crowds to behave in an orderly manner. A small army of Pinkerton guards is on duty all over the course, firmly but unobtrusively exercising control. Running is discouraged and woe betide anyone who tries to take a camera along – it is confiscated instantly.

It seems to give the spectators a feeling of security to know just how far they can go. And the one place where they are not admitted is on to the field of action – the fairways. Only the players and the caddies are allowed there. This is in marked contrast to, say, the Ryder Cup at Muirfield, where there were almost as many people inside the ropes as behind them.

I found the galleries at Augusta both knowledgeable and impartial. On the last day I was sitting in the stand overlooking the fifteenth green and its guardian lake, when along came Maurice Bembridge. He had started the day at three over par for the tournament and, as he came down the hill towards the lake, the scoreboard showed a red 3 beside his name, indicating that he was now three under par. A mental calculation revealed that he needed a level par finish for a round of 66.

I was not the only person to have accomplished this mathematical feat. As Bembridge came level with the stand everyone got up and applauded him warmly. He responded by picking up another stroke to par and finished his round with yet another birdie at the final hole. I have seldom heard such an ovation as Maurice received when this long putt dropped for a record-equalling round of 64. The applause and cheering must have lasted more than two minutes.

Maurice's effort was not enough to earn him the Green Jacket, of course, but it was a great performance. Gary Player won the tournament for the second time and had his name inscribed again on the biggest trophy I have ever seen – a model of the Augusta National Golf Club in silver.

It gets very hot in Augusta during the summer and the course is closed. But over the next months all the fairways are re-seeded, and small improvements are carried out in preparation for the band of nervous hopefuls who will turn into Magnolia Lane the following year.

For green read brown

GORDON RICHARDSON

When is a green not a green? When it's a brown – as hundreds of British and Irish golfers have found out in the Nigerian Open at the Ikoyi Club in Lagos over the thirteen years of the championship's life.

Browns – a greyish mixture of fine sand and multigrade oil whose exact recipe is kept a close secret – are a fact of golfing life in Nigeria, and for that matter The Gambia and some other neighbouring West African states. They are as different as chalk and cheese from the manicured lawns the players normally play on, but there are few complaints. For, as Scotland's Sam Torrance points out: 'They're basically a heck of a lot easier to putt on. Every one is as flat as a pancake with no hidden borrows. The hole looks bigger because of the cambered lip and even slightly off-line putts tend to fall in.'

Irishman Eamonn Darcy agrees: 'Most of the circular browns are small. You're rarely more than twenty feet from the flag, so it's almost impossible to three-putt: all you have to judge is distance and pace.'

According to the mix, browns can be made fast or slow. Heavy traffic soon makes them resemble Bank Holiday beaches, but a sweeper (if he is not snoozing behind a palm tree) is always on hand to smooth the line of every putt with a contraption whose wooden leading edge and trailing oily sacking magically remove footprints and pitchmarks.

Consequently hot streaks are common at Ikoyi. Sheffield's David Jagger rationed himself to only 21 putts when he waltzed round in 59 in a pro-am in 1973. In 1978 Sandy Lyle set a record of 124 for thirty-six holes when opening up 61, 63 en route to his maiden victory. And in February 1981 the Yorkshireman, Peter

Tupling, won with a new world record, 29 below par, aggregate of 255.

Wars across the Kenya border in Uganda and the Zambian border in Zimbabwe, and a bloody abortive coup in Nigeria, have failed to kill off Africa's Safari Golf Circuit, on which, as well as temperatures close to 100 degrees Fahrenheit and drenching humidity, day to day hazards include mosquito bites and what the locals euphemistically call 'tummy palaver', not to mention six-inch-wide columns of marching ants and the two-storey-house-sized anthills they construct – sometimes in mid-fairway.

Brian Barnes, of the short shorts and puffing briar, dominated the £220,000 circuit in 1981 despite missing the first two events. He won the Kenya and Zambian Open titles and over £15,500 in prize money to top an order of merit which saw Tupling, Gordon Brand (winner of the Ivory Coast Open over President Houphouet Boigny's home-town course of Yammoussoukro) and Darcy, winner of the Cock of the North Open at Ndola, in Zambia's Copper Belt, all earn more than £9000. In fact, no fewer than fifty-two professionals of the 110 figuring in the final order of merit won £1000 or more, which proves what a good investment the trip can be.

Barnes's wins were contrasting affairs. In Nairobi on the Muthaiga course he encountered a sudden tropical whirlwind which slashed visibility, littered greens with debris and left players spluttering and coughing – 'just like the end of the world'. Twenty-four hours later Barnes stomped angrily off the course, believing he had blown his chance. He was halfway through his third pint of lager when Bernard Gallacher took six at the last to hand his Ryder Cup pal the title.

In Lusaka the scene as Barnes rolled in the winning putt was charged with emotion. On to the green rushed Head of State Kenneth Kaunda to proclaim: 'Well done, son!' and fling his arms around Barnes, who responded: 'Thanks, Dad!'

The relationship between the two is, indeed, like that of father and son. Brian annually leads a team of pros against the President's Men over KK's private course in the grounds of State House. Brian explains ruefully: 'I've played six times and we've lost five of them. The tradition is that they don't reveal their handicaps until *after* the match – they always start pretty confident!

'We play off plus-two and they get their full stroke allowance. This time when all the scores were added up they won by 986 strokes to 1114. One Kenyan pro's 86 counted for us while they had a guy go round in a net 58 off 14!'

His Excellency, a very useful fourteen-handicapper, returned a net 65 to better Barnes's 67, despite taking time out to serve his guests personally at a luncheon on the State House lawns. This is a light-hearted affair, with match conditions stating that 'all members of the home team will act as tournament referees and their ruling on any issue is final.'

Local rules include: 'Peacocks, guinea fowl, duikers, impala etc. have the right of the course. Anyone causing injury or death to any of these birds or animals will suffer the following penalties: immediate and ignominious suspension from the State House golf course and in the case of the visiting team a detailed report of the inhuman and unsportsmanlike conduct will be submitted to the PGA with a copy to the R and A.'

The friendly relationship between Barnes and Kaunda is typical of the Safari Tour. Players normally stay as house guests of expatriate club members and firm friendships result, with hosts nursing their charges through the week with anti-malaria pills, salt tablets, stomach medicines and flasks of iced drinks.

Chummy pro-ams are plentiful with the first two rounds of the Kenya Open, a celebrity affair with Variety Club members like Dickie Henderson, Eric Sykes, Bobby Charlton, Henry Cooper and Richie Benaud helping to raise thousands of pounds for charities.

President Kaunda himself sums up: 'Good sport builds bridges between people where money and many other actions fail. The swinging of so many golf clubs in our country cannot fail to add confidence to the swing of life in our nation and to goodwill and understanding among all the people of the participating countries.'

Hazards from the sky

DERMOT GILLEECE *Irish Times*

In true missionary fashion, officials of the Golfing Union of Ireland were set upon by angry natives while attempting to play their part in promoting the game of golf in Iceland. It was a vicious onslaught, totally without warning, leaving our intrepid adventurers extremely grateful for the relative peace and calm which one associates with the game in their own islands. Let me explain how it happened.

The Union hierarchy – the president, John McInerney, and president-elect, Fred Perry – were enjoying a leisurely game on the nine-hole Ness course, situated on a peninsula about seven kilometres from Reykjavik, when suddenly the air was rent with a strange bird cry. At first it sounded not unlike a common seagull, but the Irish officials became a little concerned when this was accompanied by a rapid rat-tat-tat, such as a woodpecker might make when attacking some unfortunate tree. Attack is an apposite word, for suddenly the birds came swooping down, as an eagle might pounce on its prey. It was only with some extremely adroit footwork and wild swinging of a mid-iron by Perry that injury to both officials was averted.

Arctic terns, which migrate to this part of Iceland to breed, are dangerous birds, particularly when their nesting areas are threatened. Smaller than a seagull and with a black head and long beak, they will dive like miniature Zeroes and attack without warning.

It was only after this frightening incident that the officials learned that it is common practice at Ness for players to walk along the fairways with a club held over their heads to ward off the terns. But even experienced campaigners have sustained head injuries, while cuts to arms and legs are common.

Perry, a West of Ireland man, never at a loss for words, commented: 'Jaysus, the boys back home would get a quare shock if these lads started coming down on them in the middle of a quiet Sunday morning fourball. I'll tell you they'd make it shockin' difficult to keep your head down in the middle of a stroke!'

Despite this unfortunate incident, however, the Irish were delighted to have made an important contribution to the twenty-first European Junior Team Championship, which was the purpose of their visit. The event was staged at Grafarhol (Hill of Graves) near Reykjavik, which has the only eighteen-hole course in Iceland.

Spain won the title by beating Ireland by five and a half matches to one and a half in the final. The highlight of this match was the four and three victory by Jesus Lopez over Walker Cup player Philip Walton in the top singles. Lopez, who had been beaten by Walton in the final of the Amateur Open Championship at Torrequebrada in March, went on to win the British Boys' title in August 1981.

It cost the Icelanders £25,000 to stage the European tests and they considered it money well spent. The main objective of Reykjavik Golf Club and the Icelandic Union was to publicize golf in their own country. Despite the previous best efforts of all concerned, golf remained a poor relation to swimming, handball, football, athletics and a traditional style of wrestling called glima, as far as the Icelanders were concerned.

There are currently 2200 golfers in twenty-one clubs playing eighteen courses in Iceland, several of which are in very poor condition. Gunnar Torfason, the Reykjavik club secretary, told me: 'Our first golfers were professional people who went abroad to be educated and brought the game back to their native country. When our course was opened in 1963 we had 150 members, but the figure is now 550 – at £100 membership fee per year.

'The problem is that we have too many golfers trying to play our course during a limited season from May until October. During that period, the course is in use for up to twenty hours each day. We are forbidden by law to restrict membership, so the only option, as we see it, is to introduce an entrance fee of £200, which is double the annual subscription. But the ideal solution would be the building of more golf courses. If the European Championship succeeds in achieving this objective, then it will have been a marvellous success.'

An Italian at the court of St Andrew

PIERO MANCINELLI

It is not the easiest job in the world to write about golf in Italy. For a start there is the problem of the language: for Italian, which serves well enough for opera, has no humour. Politicians are the only people who master the complexities of Italian syntax and nobody understands them. Then, the subject matter does not help. Although many people have tried to associate golf with my country, through the Roman game of paganica, to Italians it is the most esoteric of sports.

An Italian thrown into the world of golf is an incongruity, like a dog in church or Brooke Shields drinking Coca-Cola in the Royal and Ancient Club. I had played golf discreetly from the age of ten but was not entirely prepared for my first experiences of big tournaments – Peter Thomson eating two kilos of apples each round as he won the Italian Open at Villa d'Este in 1959, or Brigitte Varangot almost finishing in another world when a rich Hispano-American turned thousands of pounds' worth of Ferrari into scrap iron by crashing it through the door of the club.

At that time I had just finished building twenty-seven holes at Olgiata, designed by my friend and teacher, C. K. Cotton. I was also starting work on Carimate, the first course for which I was solely responsible. Before the Italian Open there was an international championship for amateurs and women and the whole *belle époque* of golf was present – Francis Francis, Count John de Bendern, Julian Earl, and ex-King Leopold of the Belgians who came with his friend, John Jacobs. Also there were the tigers of the 100,000 lire Nassau, which was a lot of money in those days. I remember going into the locker room and seeing bundles of million-lire notes on the benches.

Two famous personalities in golf, one French with a reputation as a fine golfer and a terrible character, and the other American, many times champion in his own country, fought like bantam cocks. The Frenchman was also known for what the British call gamesmanship. During a match with the Swiss amateur Dillier, the Frenchman was asked to mark his ball on the green. He did so, creating in the process a deep indentation in the green right on the line of Dillier's putt. Dillier turned without saying a word and walked from the course, thereby conceding the hole and the match. In Italy we have a word rather more picturesque and rude than gamesmanship.

This was the year when golf ceased to be a pleasant diversion for me and became, slowly and fatally, my profession. At first it was just an extension of my work as an engineer. Then the company for which I was working informed me that I was to be a member of the organizing committee for the Eisenhower Trophy at Olgiata in 1964. I recall that terrible, rain-swept week as a continual test of my nerves because the whole affair was so dreadfully over-organized. Cecil B. de Mille himself could not have created a greater spectacular, with a banquet at the capital, a reception at Castel Santangelo during the last act of *Tosca*, films (using army projectors, perhaps the only ones working in the whole country), flags sodden with rain, the Royal Marines' band and the teams marching proudly – all for the peaceful, beautiful game of golf.

In the sixties we had a mini professional circuit in Italy, supported by many British players and played virtually *in camera*. When Neil Coles won the Walworth Aloyco tournament the members of Rome Golf Club were either inside playing bridge or golfing on another course. Christy O'Connor was the only player with a gallery, four priests from the Irish College. The British golf press ignored our circuit; there was just me reporting for the *Gazzetta della Sport*.

During the last Walworth Aloyco Peter Alliss fell victim to the twitch, or yips. He walked off the ninth green, removed his glove and gave it to his caddy, Romano (now the manager of a successful business). 'This is the first time I've retired in mid-round,' he told me, 'but it's ridiculous to miss two-foot putts.'

Romano asked what he should do with the bag. 'Throw it in the lake. I think the lake by the first hole is the deepest. Make it disappear.'

My next involvement in organizing a tournament was in 1971 at the Lancia d'Oro at Biella. Communications were the main problem here and I invited the local association of amateur radio hams to help. They arrived by the dozen. The only problem was that their transmissions of scores back to base were so enthusiastic that play had to be halted because of excessive decibels.

Since then I have been involved full time in golf, as course designer and journalist. At the Spanish Open of 1971 at El Prat I sympathetically followed the occasionally irrational Ettore Della Torre, who like many Italians, was later to lose his game for no reason. On the eleventh hole Della Torre pulled his approach to an adjacent fairway. Between his ball and the hole were a bunker, a stand of pine trees, another bunker and about one metre of green. Della Torre dismissed all these botanical and geological details from his mind and hit the ball straight into the hole, to the astonishment of Peter Dobereiner, who was standing with me. As an old patriot I cried: 'Bravo, Ettore!'

The player replied: 'What do you want, *Dottore*? I had to try it!' In Italy, I should explain, anyone who has been to university is universally known as '*Dottore*'. No decently-dressed visitor to Italy should be surprised at being called '*Dottore*' by porters, taxi-drivers, receptionists and waiters.

If your luggage is smart enough, and you're carrying golf clubs, you may even be addressed as '*signor conte*'. Take it from me, the best thing to do in these circumstances is to keep smiling and refrain from explaining that you are not a count. You will save on tips. Because in Italy nobody expects that a count, especially if he plays golf, will have any money.

Golf starvation

TED OSTERMANN *Golf Vertrieb*

During the summer of 1981 I received a telephone call from a prominent Japanese businessman asking if I could help him find a golf course which he could buy for the use of his countrymen living in Germany. The enquiry was logical and perfectly understandable when you reflect that more Germans than ever prefer to drive Japanese cars, try to solve their financial problems with the aid of Japanese pocket calculators and have long become Far East orientated in the field of electronic entertainment equipment. Consequently thousands of Japanese who staff their industries near Hamburg and Duesseldorf live in a golfing no-man's land.

Anyone who is familiar with Germany will understand why I had to tell the caller: 'I'm sorry, but all the money in the world can't buy a golf course here.' As far as golf is concerned Germany is an underdeveloped country. It is not only the Japanese who forget the difference between slice and hook with which they had become familiar on their domestic driving ranges. Because of the lack of public courses ambitious young German golfers are hardly ever able to experience the thrill of that easy fourth putt. Many of them will never be able to enjoy what could well become a lasting source of pleasure or even a career, because of shortsightedness and lack of understanding on the part of the German authorities.

For a long time Bernhard Langer tried to earn a living while taking forty putts a round, and more; and once he got the knack of putting, in the latter half of 1980, began to win tournaments. Before that Langer had a reputation on the professional circuit as the best supporting actor on the greens. Some of his three-putt antics were worthy of an Oscar. He would have walked any competition for the most putts.

Until 1981 German journalists had written disparagingly about the snooty game of golf; but the international deeds of twenty-four-year-old Langer forced golf on to the sports pages. When he took second place in the Open Championship at Sandwich, and then became the first German to win the German Open, beating Tony Jacklin by a stroke, golf was suddenly In. Overnight the game was as fashionable as the rumba danced by Adenauer and de Gaulle when they discovered the 'traditional friendship' between their nations.

At present there are some 50,000 golfers in Germany, out of a population of fifty-seven million, playing on fifty-four eighteen-hole courses and 106 nine-hole courses, only one of which is public. All the clubs are full to capacity, with long waiting lists. Most of the applicants face a long wait indeed before they will have an opportunity to join the swinging world of golf, unless the authorities change their tune. The official view is that there is not enough land for courses. In fact there is plenty of suitable land which could be put to profitable use for public golf.

What if Langer should develop into a national hero and symbol such as Beckenbauer became for the young soccer fans? I cannot see how another young German professional could find the encouragement to follow in Langer's footsteps. I fancy that we shall see the thirty-hour working week before we see the next one or two public courses in Germany. And how I hope that I will be proved wrong.

PART EIGHT

Rubs of the green

Out on a limb

CHRISTOPHER PLUMRIDGE

If God, as we are led to believe, made us in His image, then He failed to realize that one day we might choose to pick up a stick and take a swipe at a pebble. This lack of foresight led Him to equip us with legs and arms of equal proportions, a pair of centralized eyes, and a collection of joints and muscles which allow us to bend, twist and turn in all directions.

While this combination makes for symmetry and allows us to perform ordinary tasks such as climbing Mount Everest, jumping a five-bar gate or simply unscrewing the cap of the gin bottle, when it comes to the business of hitting the pebble with the stick it is utterly useless.

Doubtless the first man or woman to hit a pebble with a stick did so without thinking how it was done, but after a while he or she would begin to wonder why the pebble could not be hit straighter and further. Other hitters would gather round and exchange views and in between inventing the wheel and discovering fire, would draw various conclusions as to what movement would make for straight and powerful hitting of the pebble. It would be at this juncture that the pebble hitters would get the first inkling that their physiology was ill-designed for their requirements.

Today's golfer, the modern equivalent of those ancient pebble hitters, faces much the same problem. God has persisted with His design and we find ourselves embarking on the job of hitting a golf ball still stuck with those symmetrical arms, legs, eyes, muscles and joints. Thus equipped, we find that to make an efficient pass at the ball we have to make one arm longer than the other, one leg shorter than the other, stiffen the joints in one arm, concave our chests and from the tip of this contorted structure peer at the ball through one eye like a Cyclops.

All of which brings me to Severiano Ballesteros. The 1979 Open champion seems, on the face of it, to be a perfectly-structured human who, without engaging in any of these contortions, can hit the ball with a freedom that leaves the watcher open-mouthed in wonderment.

But now I can reveal to you the secret of Ballesteros's success. While I was dining with him recently, the talk came round to theories about the hitting of a golf ball. 'How,' I asked, 'do you manage to hit the ball so far?' Since Ballesteros is built like a Pamplona bull, that question may seem trite; but many bigger men still trail the young Spaniard in length from the tee. Ballesteros said nothing in reply but simply stood up and asked me to study the length of his arms.

Suddenly, as he stood there, all was clear. With his shoulders perfectly level, Ballesteros's right arm was almost two inches longer than his left. With the discovery of this physical phenomenon everything fell into place. You and I when addressing the golf ball have to drop the right shoulder to place the right hand in the correct position on the grip and also check that, in so doing, we have not pointed our shoulders left of the target, but Ballesteros can get into the correct address position by virtue of a natural defect.

Come to think of it, a hint of physical abnormality may be the difference between being a good golfer and a champion. History can provide us with some excellent examples, not least Ben Hogan. Hogan in his prime was thought to strike the ball as perfectly as is humanly possible; in the words of Gene Sarazen 'nobody covered the flag like Hogan'. What may have given Hogan the edge over his contemporaries was the fact that although naturally left-handed, he chose to play golf right-handed.

Johnny Miller is another golfer who plays right-handed while being naturally left-handed, and although his star has long since descended from the heights of 1973 to 1976, during that period he produced a brand of golf that bordered on the fantastic.

And could it be that Ed Furgol won the 1954 US Open because of this withered left arm, rather than in spite of it? Furgol's was not a natural defect but the result of a childhood accident after which the arm was badly set. Although his left arm was too short and the muscles atrophied it was permanently locked, thereby allowing him to overcome a fault which plagues thousands of golfers.

Consider too the case of Vicente Fernandez, the 1979 PGA champion. He won that title at St Andrews playing through some of the vilest weather imaginable. But Fernandez had one priceless advantage over his rivals – he was playing every stroke from a slight uphill lie simply because he was born with his right leg shorter than his left. Most golfers when playing from a slight uphill lie find themselves hitting a better shot than normal. Indeed Douglas Bader, who lost both legs in a pre-war flying accident, discovered the same. He could ensure a permanent uphill stance for every shot by simply sawing an inch or two from his right leg.

The real clincher to my theory, however, is Jack Nicklaus. Nicklaus is colour blind. This may seem like a disadvantage until you consider that at most tournaments nowadays the leader-boards show a player's figures in relation to under-par scores in red. To Nicklaus these figures appear black, thereby providing him with the mental confirmation that he is far ahead of any other player in the field.

If God wants to produce the ideal golfer then He should create a being with a set of unequal arms and likewise legs, an elbow-free left arm, knees which hinge sideways and a ribless torso from which emerges, at an angle of forty-five degrees, a stretched neck fitted with one colour blind eye stuck firmly on the left side. And please God, let it be British.

A lady of quality

MICHAEL WILLIAMS   *Daily Telegraph*

We first met, her ladyship and I, at Moor Park. In Ross Whitehead's shop to be exact. She caught my eye at once. It was not love at first sight, but there was an obvious purity about her, untouched by any other male.

I took her out on to the practice green. She was a nice weight with a good touch. She was, it soon became obvious, just what I had been looking for ever since my first love was spirited away some years before: stolen, in fact.

I bought her ladyship, an Acushnet mallet-headed putter, for £6, I think it was, and we lived together happily for many years. We had our ups and we had our downs and, here and there, on less faithful occasions, I had other mistresses. But always we came back together, seeking the touch and understanding of the blissful days.

Like the time when together we reached the final of the club knock-out. I had been there once before but that was eleven years earlier when the game, certainly on the greens, was personally fraught with less difficulty. It was a thirty-six-hole match and I will always remember the putts we sank together over the first six holes. We were as one, each confident in the other, three up at lunch.

Then the holes began to slip away. Back to two up, then one, all square, one down and now only nine to play. What I remember best were the last three holes, the match again level. At the sixteenth, the thirty-fourth, the enemy holed from a disheartening length for a four, but we followed him in from twelve feet for the half. The seventeenth, which plays longer than its yards, has never been my sort of hole, but somehow a three-iron second reached the green.

If ever there was a moment to get a birdie, this was it. We holed.

One up. The last is a short hole and from the back of the green the two of us laid the ball dead for the three and the match.

That was our finest hour together. More painful ones followed and I don't think we ever quite got on when we went abroad. I never gave her ladyship a name like Bobby Jones and his 'Calamity Jane', though calamitous moments there certainly were. Greens are not the same in foreign parts, and one or other of us would be upset by the weather or the watering, the grain or the deceptive undulations. We had our moments, but not many.

And then, for the first time, we went together to America for the 1977 Walker Cup. I could foresee some time on my hands in the week leading up to the match and it seemed a good idea to take clubs. Shinnecock Hills beckoned, and goodness knows where else, given a bit of luck and an invitation here and there.

The relationship between her ladyship and me had by this time become a trifle strained. We were missing more than we were holing, though I must say I think I was to blame. Other than a band of tape around the bottom of her grip, her ladyship had retained her figure – though her head did show some scratches, sustained on gravel and stones and the odd cuff about the ears as an iron club was thrust back into the bag.

We played together twice that September weekend and lost each time. Afterwards, while doodling round the professional's shop, I was startled to find what, for a moment, I took to be her ladyship's head lying on the counter, separated indeed from her body.

'Don't worry,' I was told. 'She's not yours. That's Steve Martin's. It broke while he was practising and it's not going to be easy to mend.'

Now I am not always a selfish man and suddenly, in a blinding moment of intuition, I saw this as the chance for her ladyship to play in the Walker Cup, something we could never possibly do together.

Her ladyship, dozing quietly with the rest of my clubs in the caddy shed, knew nothing of her impending destiny. But through Sandy Saddler, the captain, I mentioned that I thought I had the twin of Martin's broken putter. Martin carried out an examination, said no, she was too heavy and her neck was not the same either.

But when his reserve putter failed him in practice, he looked again. I renewed the offer of her ladyship's services and Martin said he would give her a trial.

It was Michael Bonallack who first predicted the news I half wanted to hear, half didn't. 'I think you've lost your putter,' he said. 'I've just walked the first nine with Martin and he's holed everything.'

When Martin came in at the end of the round, he confirmed her ladyship's willing compliance with his intentions and my one resolve now was to see her in action in the Walker Cup. It was quite a wait.

I stood behind the first green that first morning. Martin was playing with Allan Brodie. They were bunkered. Martin came out and Brodie holed. At the second Brodie's tee shot ran through. Martin chipped dead and still her ladyship waited. At the third Martin chipped in for a birdie. At the fourth the Americans drove into a bush, made a frightful mess of things and conceded the hole without asking the British to putt.

Finally, at the fifth, came the moment. Brodie putted a yard past, out came her ladyship and in went the ball. Satisfied, I moved off to leave Martin to the business of becoming one of the more successful members of an otherwise unsuccessful side. On the last afternoon her ladyship played top against Lindy Miller. There was a chance on the last green of an eight-foot putt for a halved match, but Miller holed his first for a winning three clean across the green.

Martin offered, without much enthusiasm, to return her ladyship, but I knew it was time to part. Anyway, I always have the happy days to remember.

It's aye the putting – and the putter

SAM McKINLAY

When I was young enough and rash enough to have ambitions in tournament golf there was always one moment of truth in every match I played – when my opponent took out his putter on the first green.

If it was steel-shafted and shiny, bret-new from the pro's shop, I relaxed, especially if it was one of those new-fangled implements that look like nothing so much as what you use to pull down a sash window.

If it was hickory-shafted with a rusty bent-neck blade, and it cuddled into my opponent's hands like an old friend, I was immediately wary, because then it was a case of like meeting like and there were days when I rather fancied my own expertise with my rusty, trusty Pipe-brand ancient.

It was doubtless an unwarranted attitude, for there are some splendid players who use shiny putters of stainless steel, such as the Benny with its grooved sole that used to be a deadly weapon in the large hands of players such as James Bruen, one of those bulky men who have a touch like Lindrum on the green.

There are, too, many notable putters who use the 'window pole' type I profess to despise, one of the best of them being Bob Charles, the king of left-handers; but his club is, I think, brass-headed and that is a kindly metal. Certainly in his hands it is a brazen serpent that stings lethally.

Bobby Locke, who was possibly the best putter of his generation, used a rusty Gem blade, but he could probably have holed putts using an umbrella and a Bath bun.

My thoughts turned to putting and putters when not long ago I played in Ayrshire with a very old friend and opponent whom I had first played against in a championship at Balgownie,

Aberdeen, in the late twenties. We had met from time to time since but had not played together, as I could recall, for all those years. On the first green he missed a tiddler, which he never used to do, and what is more he missed it with the same putter he had used against me more than forty years earlier. For the record, as if it were worth recording, I holed a clubhouse yarder on the first green with the same putter I had used against him at Balgownie.

He has never in all those years swerved in his allegiance to his putter – a rusty, bent-neck instrument that is almost the twin of my own. I can claim no such fidelity. Once or twice, 'when in disgrace with fortune and men's eyes', I have dallied with other putters – once, may I be forgiven, with an aluminium-headed monster, once or twice with a brass-headed cleek out of a famous Kinghorn forge, and once with a replica of my own, the last of a consignment made up by a skilly clubmaker at St Andrews to satisfy two American professionals who had seen, handled, admired and envied my own putter during one of my visits to the United States. But always I returned to my first love and I have no doubt, in the old Scots phrase, 'it will see me out'.

The old caddy knew what he was saying when he proclaimed: 'It's aye the putting.' He might have added: 'It's aye the putter.' It is possibly the most individual of all the clubs in the bag and certainly the best of the pros would list it, along with the driver and the wedge, as the most important. After all, even the best players use their putter more often than any other club, and although many of their tally of putts are merely tap-ins they will probably play at least one stroke on each green that requires skill, touch, nerve, and a club in which they have full confidence. That is more than can be said of any other club in the bag.

You will gather that I have a great affection for the old putters, the ones forged from mild steel which I think was known as Waverley metal. They seem to me to make a most satisfying sound when they strike the ball, a ringing click if that is not a contradiction in terms, as against the dull little thud of so many modern contraptions.

But just because a putter is old is no guarantee that it is good. Once I was given a genuine Willie Park head by the late Rex

Hartley, a real treasure. I had it shafted and set forth to be cock of the walk. And I don't think I ever holed a single putt worth recording with this priceless putter. The reason was ill to seek and I did not find it for many years, long after I had jettisoned the gift. The wisest of clubmakers, Laurie Auchterlonie, told me that many of the old putter heads had a basic fault. The hosel was drilled rather haphazardly, and unless the shaft was perfectly shaped and inserted with uncommon care the result was a failure because the club would have a built-in hook or be permanently offset. At least the modern putter is a model of precise engineering.

So, if you acquire, as two of my golfing friends have recently, an ancient putter from some ancient bag, get it vetted by an expert. It may look good, it may feel good, it may even swing beautifully – but you'll putt 'like an auld sweetie-wife'.

I tried, in my own blundering way, to coax the shaft of one of those ancient putters into a Musselburgh bend so that my hands in the address would point not down the shaft but at the centre of the blade and therefore at the ball. But all I managed to do was to crack the shaft slightly, so now the owner has had to bind it with whipping.

At that he's in the best of company. Bobby Jones's 'Calamity Jane' had to be whipped some inches above the blade to secure the shaft, and it was surely the most sincere kind of flattery that, when his putter was copied for commercial sale, the copies also had whipping in the same place, although the shafts were flawless.

Fluke or skill

JOHN PARGETER *Newcastle Journal*

Is it skill, is it luck, is it a combination of both? And are there a whole lot of other factors to be taken into consideration as well when we consider the ace, or hole in one?

Many a rabbit has succeeded in achieving the feat, whereas

thousands of top-class players have not. Invariably when an unusual ace is reported, sports writers turn to the record books to find out if it has been done previously, and inevitably they are astounded at what they discover.

Two incidents in my own experience come readily to mind. John Jacobs was invited to a topping-out ceremony at the Gosforth Park Hotel just north of Newcastle-upon-Tyne. A special tee had been erected on top of the building sixty-six feet up, and a hole cut in the lawn below some ninety yards away. Jacobs was to play thirty-five balls at the target to raise money for the Variety Club of Great Britain, several firms having sponsored the challenge, and some £2500 was raised. Then, with his thirtieth hit, the ball went into the hole and the hotel owners acclaimed the feat by handing over another £1000. It is doubtful if a hole-in-one has ever been achieved from such a lofty spot.

In contrast, I recall a most frustrating view of a hole-in-one at Bishop Auckland, County Durham – a view which at that time could have made golfing history. It happened during the Northern Counties' Ladies Championship, and Durham, who were the hosts on this occasion, had gone through to the last day unbeaten. They were then due to play Cheshire.

I went along with a Tyne-Tees TV crew to film each member of the Durham team individually, and was standing behind the short tenth planning film of the Durham girl about to play, but the Cheshire girl was on the tee first so the camera was switched off. She promptly put it in the hole, right under the camera lens, and had the camera been running it would have been the first hole-in-one to be televised.

Britain holds one hole-in-one world record: for a brother and sister holing on the same green one after the other. It happened at the eighteenth at Sidmouth in Devon. Janet Bell, aged twenty-five, went first, using a two wood from the 253-yard ladies' tee, then Alistair, aged nineteen, used his driver for the 291-yard men's tee. It is a blind hole, and they were astounded to find both balls in the hole.

When a twelve-year-old, Neil McDiermid, sank his tee shot with a three wood at Stocksfield, a course in my neck of the woods, I was astonished to discover that it was by no means a record. In fact, the youngest gentleman to do it was only five at the time. He is Coby Orr from Littleton in Colorado. He did it in 1975 at the Riverside Golf Course in San Antonio, Texas, where the fifth hole measures 103 yards. Another player, aged six years and twenty-one days, holed out in Melbourne, Australia, in 1979. One, aged six years and seven days, succeeded in Martinsville, West Virginia, in 1968, and it would appear that the record for a girl is held by Rebecca Chase, who holed out when she was eight. That happened in 1977 in Oregon.

In Britain, as far as is known, the youngest to score an ace was one Harry Pratt when seven and a half. He sank his tee shot at the 111-yard sixth hole at Thurlestone in 1974. This prompted more research into *The Golfer's Handbook* – commonly referred to as the Golfer's Bible – where many of the facts above and those which follow have over the years been faithfully chronicled by its editors.

In 1951 a competition was held over several days in New York where 1409 players, all of whom had done a hole-in-one, played at short holes on three of the city's courses. Each player was allowed five shots, giving an aggregate of 7045 strokes. None holed-in-one. In fact, the nearest ball finished three and a half inches from the hole.

In 1940 an American professional, Harry Gonder, stood for sixteen hours twenty-five minutes hitting 1817 balls trying to do a 160-yard hole-in-one. He had two official witnesses and caddies to tee-up and retrieve the balls and to count the strokes. His 1756th shot struck the hole but stopped an inch away. That was the nearest he came.

America has come up with a statistical analysis claiming that the odds for a male professional or top amateur to achieve a hole-in-one are 3708 to 1: for a female professional or top amateur they are 4658 to 1: for an average player they are 42,952 to 1.

But be not disheartened. Over the 447-yard tenth at the Miracle Hill course in Omaha, one Bob Mitera got a hole-in-one. It has been done by three ninety-year-old gentlemen, and Norman Manley of Long Beach in California has done it forty-three times.

If you really want the answer to that original question, how about the gentleman who over-clubbed, went out of bounds, hit a rock and saw the ball rebound on to the green fifty yards away, then go into the hole. Skill or luck?

'They also serve who only pace the yardage . . .'

BILL ELLIOTT   *Daily Star*

Suffolk Road, Birkdale, is an unlikely place to figure in the legend and folklore of golf. An ordinary little street with just twenty-eight ticky-tacky houses, for the past 100 years it has been the home of ordinary working-class Lancastrians. What Suffolk Road has that no modern city planner could provide is one of the greatest backyards in the world.

It is called Royal Birkdale; and with its hills and hollows, wind and sun, it rightly lays claim to being one of the finest links courses.

But in the hungry 1930s Royal Birkdale was seen by the little lads who were growing up in Suffolk Road not so much as a fusion of God and man's art as a chance to earn some cash. A day spent humping a gentleman's bag meant an extra loaf in the house by tea-time. In the fullness of time it meant also that Suffolk Road was able to lay claim to a significant share in no less than eight Open Championship victories. Jacky Leigh caddied twice for Peter Thomson when he won the Open. Teddy Dalsall guided Johnny Miller to victory and Albert Fyles won with Tom Weiskopf. Overshadowing them all is Albert's brother Alfie Fyles, who has known the thrill of walking to the last green and certain victory *four* times.

His first taste of this sweetest of wines came with Gary Player at Carnoustie in 1968; but it is with Tom Watson that Fyles himself has been able to reach out and touch greatness. Three times –

Carnoustie 1975, Turnberry 1977 and Muirfield 1980 – Fyles has coaxed and cursed his American master to victory. The most significant win for Alf, and for caddies everywhere, came in 1975.

'I've had some great moments, but that win with Tom gave me the greatest professional satisfaction because he had never played golf over here before, never even been in the country, so it was a hell of a challenge. Any chance we had of winning seemed to go by the board completely when Tom arrived too late for even a practice round.'

Instead of feeling his way around Carnoustie for a couple of days, Watson had to turn to Fyles and say: 'Alf, I'm gonna have to lean on you this week. Hard.'

And he did! Fyles's response, meanwhile, provided the perfect answer to those people who think a caddy's job is no more than a porter's role at a railway station.

'Tom not only asked me the yardage on every shot and where the best place to put the ball was, he asked me what club he should take. The man is a genius at the game but I've no doubt that a good fifty-five per cent of that Open win was down to me,' he says with pride.

Yet the greatest sporting double act since Pat Taafe and Arkle almost ended right there in Carnoustie. The trouble was the money Watson passed over to Fyles. There wasn't enough of it.

'I thought he was a bit mean at that time and so the next year I caddied for Gary Player again,' says Fyles simply.

That was in 1976, the year Miller won by six strokes from Jack Nicklaus and a young Spaniard called Ballesteros. Watson missed the cut.

'I got a Christmas card and several letters from Tom before the next Open at Turnberry but I knew my worth and I was not going to budge,' recalls Fyles. 'Actually it was Tom's lovely wife Linda who got us back together again. She asked me to have a word with Tom and when she smiles I can't refuse her anything.'

Tom and Alf talked, a new deal was struck between player and caddy and Alfie Fyles took a giant stride into the game's history, for it was at Turnberry in 1977 that we witnessed the greatest head-to-head duel of modern times.

On one side Watson. On the other, the King, Jack Nicklaus. After two rounds they were level. In the third they both shot 65. It was marvellous, magical stuff and few of us dared hope that the final round could be anything but an anti-climax. Fyles agreed.

'After I came in from that third round I said to friends that I'd just been part of the greatest golf you could see and that there was no way they could repeat that. But they did. Saturday they were just as good.

'I've never seen a crowd get so excited. In fact, at the ninth tee Jack and Tom sat down and told officials they wouldn't carry on unless the galleries behaved themselves. The really crucial point for us came at the fifteenth where Nicklaus was fourteen feet from the hole while Tom was off the green and a long way away.

'When Tom's ball rolled in for a birdie I saw Nicklaus rock back on his heels as though he'd been slapped in the face. He knew then that this Open was not his.'

It almost wasn't Alfie Fyles's Open either, for before he was to reach the eighteenth green the stocky little man with the rattling laugh was to be half trampled to death.

'After Tom played his approach shot at the last, the crowd went wild again trying to get close to the green. A pro's bag is heavy – and suddenly I found myself flat on my back with feet hitting me everywhere,' he said.

That incident left Fyles with a permanent memento of an Open victory – the only one he has, as caddies are not thought by the R and A to be worthy of a keepsake.

'Someone stamped on my right wrist so hard they ground my watch right into my skin. I've got the scar and the lump to this day, but it's a small price because I feared for my life at one point.'

The 1980 victory at Muirfield was a mundane affair compared to Turnberry but once again the man from Kansas and the man from Southport proved themselves to be in a different class. 'We make a good team,' smiles Alf. 'I'm fifty-five now and the only man who makes me want to carry on lugging those bloody great bags around is Watson. He's so solid, so good, that I believe we'll win at least two more Opens before I have to pack this daft job in.'

A daft job that started for Alf when, as an eight-year-old, he used to hurry from his paper round to caddy at Birkdale for nine old pence a round and threepence off the caddy master. He earns more now, but still not a lot. Offer the job, the hours, the conditions and the pay to many people and they would run laughing for the nearest dole.

'Aye, in the old days we often had to bed down behind a green somewhere. We used to call it 'staying with Mrs Greenfields'. If you wanted a wash you stopped at the first pond. It's better nowadays but I suppose we are still modern gypsies. There's something in my blood that makes me want to be a travelling man.

'But you'd have to be even dafter than me to do this job for the money!'

Advantage golf

LEWINE MAIR

For many a games player, golf seems to be the natural sequel to tennis. Not only is it perhaps easier for some to grow old gracefully in golf than in tennis but, for the more competitive, switching to a game in which, as recently as 1969, Jack Cannon won the Scottish Amateur Championship when he was fifty-three years of age, offers real possibilities of playing to a high standard.

Good tennis players often make good golfers, with Ellsworth Vines, who won both Wimbledon and the US Open in 1932 and went on to reach the semi-final of the PGA Championship, the most celebrated example. Rod Laver has been a low single-figure man for some time and, indeed, golf has proved so irresistible to him over the years that, when he joined Jack Kramer's tennis circus, it had to be written into his contract that he would not spend more than a certain percentage of his time on the golf course. Left-handed in tennis, Laver is a right-handed golfer, just as his fellow Australian, Ken Rosewall, is right-handed in tennis and left-handed in golf.

Althea Gibson and Winnie Wooldridge, nee Shaw, are other
tennis luminaries who have become more than useful golfers, as is
Bob Falkenburg, who has played in our Amateur Championship.
However, I doubt if, with the pressure of modern sport, there will
ever be anyone to match Lottie Dod, a young lady who, at the turn
of the century, made it to the number one spot in both tennis and
golf.

Labelled by Lord Aberdare the first 'infant prodigy' of tennis,
Lottie Dod was fifteen when she played at Wimbledon in 1887. She
won the championship that year – and did so every year until 1893,
save on the two occasions she was unable to compete.

Bored with playing tennis at the tender age of twenty-one,
Lottie Dod turned to golf. Within two years she was playing for
England against Ireland at Portrush and, in 1904, she won the
British Women's Championship at Troon, defeating May Hazlet
on the last green in what must have been the closest final she had
known in either of her chosen sports.

Paradoxically, although Miss Dod was to be remembered in
tennis for the strength of her smash and volley – unusual armoury in
the game of a Victorian woman – she yet served under-arm on the
grounds that an overarm service placed too great a strain on a
woman player. In golf, Miss Dod excelled with her woods, while her
powers of recovery were by all accounts uncanny for one of her sex.

Cecil Leitch, the quadruple British champion who has known all
but a couple of her sister champions in an event that dates back to
1893, remembers Lottie Dod as a most unassuming person who
was, as she sees it, an even greater sportswoman than Babe
Zaharias. Tennis and golf apart, she was, one gathers, a champion
skater, a skilful archer, a fine billiards player and 'a noteworthy
member of the Alpine club'.

The Babe, in fact, did not wait to start tennis until her retirement
from golf. Rather, she took it up in 1940 while she was waiting to
be declared an amateur by the United States Golf Association, that
body having made her a professional back in 1935 on account of
the professional athletics to which she had taken after her success
in the 1932 Olympics.

Her husband, George, a celebrated wrestler, took her for tennis lessons to one Eleanor Tennant, a coach who has had such as Maureen Connolly under her wing.

It was the declared ambition of The Babe to work her way to the top in one more sport – and the superhuman effort she put into her tennis can be gauged from the following extract out of her biography: 'I played as many as sixteen and seventeen practice sets in a day. There was hardly a day when I didn't wear holes in my socks, and I ran the soles off one pair of tennis shoes after another.'

In 1941, Eleanor Tennant declared that her pupil was ready for the women's tennis circuit. The Babe sent in her entry for the Pacific South West Championship, but, as had happened in golf, she was turned down on the grounds that she had once been involved in sport as a professional. From that day, The Babe never touched a racket. 'It's not enough for me just to be able to play a game,' she explained, simply. 'I have to be able to try for championships.'

In 1943 she was deemed an amateur golfer and, through 1946 and '47, won fifteen tournaments in a row by way of a prelude to her victory in the British Women's Championship at Gullane. Though there was no financial necessity for her to turn professional, the offers sired by that string of successes were too good to turn down. She was in at the start of the Ladies' Professional Golf Association tour and, as the world knows, dominated that circuit in its early years, winning four All-American Opens.

Althea Gibson is yet another good all-round games player – she could apparently have reached the top in soft-ball or baseball – to couple golf with tennis. Said to have all the muscular co-ordination of the Kenyan Olympic athletes, Althea Gibson made the transition from one sport to the other after winning the second of her two Wimbledon titles in 1958.

She had gone back to the USA determined to further 'a better relationship between negro and white America' and, as part of her campaign, had linked up with Karol Fageros in an exhibition tour for the Harlem Globetrotters. Her tennis was still superb – but the climate of America was not ready for such a mixed tour and the fact that it was not a success made her restless.

Five years later she started competitive life anew as a golf professional. She did not make much of an impact for the first four years but, in 1967, succeeded in finishing third behind Clifford Ann Creed and Ruth Jessen in the Pacific Classic. 'All I know,' she said after that display, 'is that I'm going to keep on trying until I win one of these things.'

In 1970 she almost made it. She had begun with rounds of 71 and 68 in the Immke Buik tournament to open up a four-shot lead but, in the final round, slipped to a 77. When it came to a play-off with the former American Women's Open Champion, Mary Mills, she lost out, the difference being that where Miss Mills, having come from behind, had her tail up, Althea Gibson was still dwelling on the chances she had let slip.

In the seventies, Winnie Wooldridge is the player who springs to mind when the subject of golfing tennis players comes up. Winner of Junior Wimbledon in 1964 and ranked number three in Britain in 1971, a year in which she reached the quarter-finals at Wimbledon, Winnie took a couple of golf lessons as a child, but only began to evince a real interest in the game after she had more or less dropped out of serious tennis.

Asked about the advantages of going into golf via tennis, Winnie, who now has a handicap of four, replied that the sense of timing developed in tennis was a definite asset. The short game, she said, had come the more easily to her, with fairway woods proving something of a stumbling block – 'I still have trouble getting a good flight on the ball.' All of which has been in direct contrast to the findings of her tennis-playing husband, Keith, who, when he first tried his hand at golf, found himself far more at ease over the longer shots.

She is aware that there are those who think she is a serious golfer, but she insists that the way in which she plays isn't serious to her. 'To have been serious in one sport,' she declares, 'is quite enough.'

With the exception of The Babe, there are no notable instances of golfers turned tennis players. There are, though, plenty of well-known golfers who dabble in tennis. The American women professionals play tennis between tournaments as a means of relaxation, with Amy Alcott and Susie McAllister just two among them who, at the outset of their careers, had had difficulty in deciding whether to come down on the side of tennis or golf. And then, of course, there is Jack Nicklaus. Tennis to him has obvious therapeutic value. For an hour or so after he lost the 1972 Open at Muirfield by one shot to Lee Trevino and so missed out for another year on his dream of the Grand Slam in a single summer, the great man was to be seen knocking back not drinks but forehands in a friendly singles on the court behind the Greywalls Hotel.

Know the course and you know the man

PETER DOBEREINER   *The Guardian*

Laughing at other people's troubles is one of the less noble human characteristics, although an affectionate smile was perhaps permissible on the occasion when Eamonn Darcy complained that he was suffering from a terrible pain in the right shoulder.

'I can hardly lift my right arm,' he said, and all the while he was using the right arm in question to massage his left shoulder.

We lesser mortals who have not been favoured in the lottery of life and been born outside Ireland can never quite come to terms with the Irish habit of disdaining pedantic detail.

'Isn't this a one-way street?'

'Shure and it is,' says the taxi driver, 'but it's bloody miles the other way.' This true incident illustrates what we might define as the Irish doctrine of greater logic.

The Irish habit of questioning the essential value of the 'do's and don'ts' of life has greatly enriched the game of golf. Take the case of the late Jimmy Bruen, a highly intelligent and educated man who certainly knew the right way to play golf according to the tablets of Holy Writ delivered to the world by Harry Vardon and Ben Hogan.

'Pronating the wrist and swinging in a plane inclined at forty-seven degrees may be all very well for them,' said Bruen, or words to that effect, 'But what works for me is this . . .'

So saying he hit the ball 300 yards with an action which students of anatomy claim to this day was impossible.

Then came Joe Carr, who threw the text books on the fire and won four Amateur Championships without giving a thought to how he was doing it. If he wanted the ball to go a long way, he gave it a skelp with 'that thing with a lump of wood on the end of it.'

If he had to play a delicate run-up he took his delicate run-up club and let nature take its course. Inevitably, they got at him. 'Look, Joe, you're an international figure, going off to play the US Masters and all, and you're an ambassador for Ireland. You really must conform to the niceties of correct golfing style.'

Joe started counting how many knuckles he was showing at address and from that day to this his best performance has been fifth in the scratch medal at Sutton.

As for Darcy, his action is unique and stems, I believe, from having spent his formative years playing at Delgany, the only vertical course in the world. The first time I played there I was loth to set off without a team of Sherpas.

Know the course and you know the man. Darcy learnt to pick up the club as if snatching a pound note out of a grate with a pair of tongs, because at Delgany if you try a classical take-away, swinging the club around the body, you simply stub the club head into the mountain.

You have only to see Jimmy Kinsella hit one shot and you can guess his early history. A young boy and keen on golf he would spend every spare minute with a club in his hand. However, his mother always warned him as he went out: 'Mind you don't get wet, Jimmy.' Being a dutiful son, and living in Ireland, this presented a problem which Jimmy solved by learning to play golf in a telephone box without benefit of a backswing.

Des Smyth is a mystery. When I first saw him play he looked like a windmill trying to turn itself inside out with the biggest overswing you ever saw. At times he was in danger of knocking the ball off its tee with his backswing. These days he is almost – dare I use the word? – orthodox. He is also the best putter in Europe; and I set out to visit his club to discover the secret of his mastery of the black art.

I asked a local to direct me to Laytown and Bettystown and wound up spending two days with a charming companion known as Betty, the best lay in town. So I never did find the secret. Not that one anyway.

Christy O'Connor is a hopeless golfer. He has no idea of the niceties of style or the conventions of the game. As we all know, in order to hit a shot of 160 yards you first have to know that the distance is 160 yards, a fact which is fed to you by your caddy who has measured the course at dawn with a surveyor's wheel. Armed with that information you now refer to your clubbing table (many superstars do this from memory – clever fellows) and read off 'six iron'.

O'Connor is completely disorganized, and all he does is look at the flag and guess. Then, according to how he's feeling, he takes any club from driver down to wedge and hits the ball a yard from the hole. I once saw him go through the bag, taking one club after another and hitting the green with all of them. Ben Crenshaw watched this performance and reeled away a broken man.

Harry Bradshaw was worse. At least O'Connor looks like a golfer as he nips a driver shot out of a cuppy lie and sends the ball boring under the wind to its distant target. Bradshaw looked as if he was hoeing potatoes – and he dressed for the part.

Worse, he did not even use matching clubs. You never saw such a collection of old rubbish as he had in his bag when he beat Billy Casper out of sight in a challenge match at Portmarnock. At that time Casper was in his prime and undoubtedly the best player in the world.

These days, what with junior training schemes and a John Jacobs golf centre in Dublin, Irish golf is under threat of being moulded into the standard stereotype. For that reason I am heartened by the sight of that young Ronan Rafferty. He has no idea of how to hold the club, he stands to the ball all wrong, he tells experts who try to put him right to go and jump in the lake.

If he keeps on doing it all wrong it is just possible that Ireland will soon have another world-beater on its hands.

Time for a change of life

PAT WARD-THOMAS *Country Life*

A golfing acquaintance recently declared that he had reached the change of life. He was, of course, referring to his golf and not to a bizarre circumstance of nature. When I sought explanation he said that the time had come when he was inclined to remember the good shots in a round rather than the bad, thereby achieving some consolation for his efforts, however paltry the overall outcome might be.

This was surprising. The last time we had played in the same match his attitude had been quite different. He had played far below his best until about the turn, when he produced a remarkable recovery stroke. The ball was on a steep, downhill, sandy lie. Between it and the flag, no more than twenty yards away, was a deep bunker, above which was a sheer little shelf to the edge of the green. It would be hard to conceive a more testing stroke: it had to be thrown up very steeply so that it would land softly. The slightest under- or over-hit would be fatal.

Gary Player, as skilled in shots from sand as anyone I have seen, could not have played the shot better. It fell gently and rolled to within inches of the hole. Whereupon his partner remarked that it made up for some of the previous errors. But the hero would have none of it, declaring that nothing could really compensate for them. From a practical viewpoint he was right; but why, as he came to realize later, not savour the triumphs, few though they may be, and forget the tragedies?

Many golfers never progress beyond this stage and sensibly

recognize that in all probability they never will. In a way they are to be envied because they return to the clubhouse not dissatisfied with their round. Perhaps their driving was steadier than usual, they may have mastered a hole that normally defeated them, one or two long putts may have fallen, maybe a bunker shot finished dead or a rare victory was won against an old rival.

A few such happy moments are sufficient to make their day even though they may have taken an awful number of strokes. They will have crowned the joy of treading smooth turf, the feel of the summer breeze, the music of birdsong, the sense of escape from mundane reality and the pleasure of being with friends. And when the round is done, how eagerly they look for someone to whom they can impart the glad tidings.

Occasionally it happens that the listener is a much more accomplished golfer and is equally anxious to unburden himself, but for very different reasons. He is seeking a sympathetic ear into which he can bemoan the strokes that spoiled his day. 'It's incredible,' he will say, 'but I had a six at the eighth, the easiest hole on the course, fluffed a chip and took three putts. Admittedly, my five-iron to the eleventh was pushed into that bunker, but it didn't have to finish in a heelmark. You know how well I've putted lately – well, I missed three from inside four feet. The greens are a bit rough, but 78 was terrible the way I was hitting the ball.' The permutations of misfortune, real or imagined, are infinite.

The victim of this recital, having no idea of how many strokes he himself had taken, could retort that he would happily settle for so few problems and would give anything to go round in 78. If ever he did pass such a landmark he would be in ecstasy, but if thereafter he did so fairly often he, too, would probably find himself dwelling overmuch on his mistakes, thinking that the 78 should have been 75, and so on, down the scale. Once a golfer has reached the stage where horizons are clearly defined and ambition sharpened, he is less likely to be satisfied with his handiwork.

Wise is the golfer who remembers that every round, however low the score, includes one or two shots that are not perfectly struck. For the great player they may only be slight errors of timing or judgement, but a matter for regret nonetheless. Accustomed as the tournament golfer is to striking the great majority of his strokes truly, he will naturally recall the few that were not, but will accept them as part of the unforeseeable day-to-day variations of form. The club golfer who is often restricted to one weekly round or less finds such a philosophy hard to acquire.

A case of the 'yips'

BEN WRIGHT *Financial Times*

I am regularly assured by the editors of the more successful golf magazines that it is instructional material alone that really sells their products in any number. Just as surely, book publishers would hardly flood the market with instructional books if they didn't think they could sell them. Unfortunately, none of these volumes or articles, however expert they might be, tells the victim either how to fight off the 'yips' or 'twitch' on the putting green. If any golfing or medical expert is ever able to come up with a cure for either of these insidious plagues that have ruined the careers of legendary professionals and humble hackers alike surely a fortune awaits him.

In October 1980 I had the opportunity to interview Bernhard Langer, at twenty-three years of age easily the best-ever golfer to come out of Germany, after his brilliant victory by five strokes in the Dunlop Masters Tournament at St Pierre Golf and Country Club in Chepstow. I was subsequently reminded by Jack Foster, a senior consultant neurologist in Newcastle-upon-Tyne, that Langer appears to be unique in that, by all accounts including his own, he appears to be the only top-class golfer ever to have clearly beaten the dreaded 'yips'.

I have to admit that I was too embarrassed to ask him to go into details about this extraordinary feat, because there is an unwritten law in golfing circles that the probing of a delicate area like the 'yips' or even shanking is absolutely taboo. I had to be satisfied with the engaging Langer's simplistic explanation that all his problems had been solved when he paid a fiver for a second-hand putter he found in a bin in professional Clive Clark's shop at Sunningdale. I had thrown away a priceless chance to enlighten a huge golfing audience hungry for a far more complicated explanation.

In an expert diagnosis of the 'yips' in *World Medicine Magazine* in 1977 entitled 'Putting on the Agony', Foster quoted Sir William Gowers, one of the nineteenth century's most articulate and revered neurologists, describing occupational neuroses as 'a group of maladies in which certain symptoms are excited by the attempt to perform some often-repeated muscular action, commonly one that is involved in the occupation of the sufferer. Other acts do not excite the symptom and are not interfered with. The most frequent symptom is spasm in the part which disturbs or prevents the due performance of the intended action.'

Foster points out that it is the ever-increasing financial rewards earned by skilled practitioners of golf that have created mental pressures which in turn have produced 'a new form of occupational cramp akin to the craft palsies described by Gowers and his contemporaries'.

Ben Hogan, Sam Snead and the late Henry Longhurst would know exactly what Sir William Gowers was getting at. Hogan was forced out of the game by such spasms at the height of his legendary powers. Snead, in order to survive, had to putt doubled over, facing the hole, his putter to one side of feet placed together, his hands far apart on the shaft in the so-called 'sidewinder' style. Longhurst gave up the game in disgust when the authorities cruelly banned the croquet-style putting that had allowed him to fight off the dreaded 'yips'.

Gowers grouped together the 'craft palsies' of the writer, violinist, pianist, harpist, zither player, seamstress, telegraphist, painter, artificial flower maker, turner, watchmaker, engraver, mason, smoker, shoemaker, milker and money counter or teller. So golfers and the 'yips' are far from unique. In Foster's words: 'The effective movement is skilled, i.e. it has been carefully learned and often performed, frequently after hours of assiduous practice.

The attempt to initiate the learned motor skill immediately triggers the spasm and leads to disintegration.'

Foster disappointingly concludes with 'God help you!' for there is no medical remedy for the 'yips'. In the case of players like Langer, the problem is surely entirely in the mind. But for lesser mortals the remedy may lie close at hand, namely in getting the mixture right.

First published in the *Financial Times*, Saturday 22 November 1980.

Hazards of the links

JOCK MacVICAR   *Daily Express*

Most of the time golf is a battle against yourself. As you lace up your shoes with quivering hands on medal day, try not to look at the out-of-bounds fence down the right-hand side of the first fairway, and start back in horror at the very mention of the shank. You have enough on your mind without worrying about other card-wrecking possibilities. On occasions, however, you succumb not to your own frailties, but to the outside agency. Take the Belleisle bull and the Kings Course caddy.

It was during the 1981 Coca-Cola Tournament at Ayr Belleisle that a couple of cheerful Scottish professionals, George and Angus McKay, were the targets of a runaway bull. The beast had broken loose from a field behind Rabbie Burns's cottage in Alloway, and spied the McKays on the fifth green.

George was over a five-foot putt when the bull made its move, and Angus, deciding on this occasion that safety was more relevant than etiquette, let out a yell as his playing partner was about to draw back his putter. 'Look out, George,' roared Angus, 'he's coming straight for us!'

George jerked up his head, spotted the animal, and immediately agreed the putt could wait. Seconds later the McKays were cowering in a nearby toilet, with the snorting bull prowling round the green. Fortunately the resourceful course superintendent, Harry Diamond, had seen the players' predicament and eventually managed to persuade the beast to return to its field behind the Bard's cottage. Gingerly the McKays crept out of their hideaway, and George, to his credit, holed the five-footer.

'The funny thing,' said Angus later, 'was that the bull never actually went on to the green. I don't think it was an Ayrshire bull, but it must have been Ayrshire trained!'

Bill Watson, former captain of the Professional Golfers Association and Whitecraigs professional for many years, was involved in a potentially less dangerous but considerably more damaging incident during the Seniors Championship at Gleneagles Hotel a few years ago.

Bill had shot a 69 in the first round, and was about to launch into his second over the King's Course when he caught sight of his caddy weaving towards the first tee. Clearly the man had not recovered from celebrating his boss's opening round, and by the time the pair of them had reached the seventh tee Bill was seven over fours and the caddy still more than one over the eight.

Watson, never one to maintain diplomatic silences, had lost two balls during this horrific spell, and on the seventh fairway the lurching caddy was shown the yellow card and warned to keep his distance. By then Bill had good reason to believe he was better not to ask for advice. At one hole, when asked for the distance of a shot, the caddy replied falteringly, 'One hundred and seventy yards, sir. Every bloody shot on this course is one hundred and seventy yards.'

Commendably, Watson kept his composure and covered the remaining holes in level par for a 77. But it was the caddy's last job at Gleneagles. At the end of it the yellow card was replaced by a red one, and the wretched bag-carrier staggered off to the nineteenth hole, never to be disturbed again.

Dispensing justice without venom

BOB SOMMERS   *United States Golf Association*

The southwestern United States is a dry and arid place, unsuited for habitation except by reptiles who come to breathe the clean, pure air or perhaps simply warm themselves in the sun, and golfers, an unsettled lot driven by perverse nature to periodic fits of distemper.

On a bright and sunny morning, as the warming sun approached apogee, a resident rattlesnake poked his head above ground, sniffed the air to find if the morning mist had flown, and settled himself for a day of contemplation. Squirming to a comfortable state in a bed of soft and yielding sand, he wiggled his rattles to be sure they had retained their proper E sharp tone overnight (he was blessed with perfect pitch), rested his head on his coils, and soon the soft sounds of sawn wood drifted across the desert. Ah, bliss.

Alas, it was not to be. Lost in a dream, he had barely entwined with his lady love when his peace was shattered by the thud of a foreign missile falling to the ground dangerously nearby. 'What's this?' he cried. He jerked his head high and craned his neck in alarm. The thought of a meteor shower crossed his mind, but as he squinted his eyes against the glare he dismissed the possibility that a heavenly body had disturbed his slumber, for there, a yard or so away, lay the object – shiny, white, perfectly round and dented symmetrically.

'Good grief,' he muttered, 'another golfer. And a woman, at that.'

Now he had nothing against women really: he was rather fond of a number of them, but they do have their place and he believed, like Tom Weiskopf, that their place was not on a golf course. If the miscreant who had interrupted his morning siesta thought he planned to lie docile while she blasted sand into his eyes in the act of extracting her ball, well she had another think coming.

He lowered his profile, so to speak, and hunkered down low while the culpritess walked sprightly into the sand pile. As she drew back her club, he thrust his head to a great height, wiggled his rattles and flicked his tongue menacingly.

A screech, followed by a shower of sand, and he was alone once more in his couch.

But not for long. Another female joined the first, and now they were in heated discussion, occasionally pointing towards him. He heard one say that she would stand by with a rake in the event that danger threatened. He hadn't counted on that. After all, he meant no bodily harm; just to frighten away the intruder so he could dream sweet dreams of amour.

After a few minutes of agitated discussion, he could see that the females were determined to carry on with their match, but at the same time he could see they were terribly troubled. Didn't want to go against the Rules of Golf, he supposed. Now the rattler hadn't survived these many years living on a golf course without learning a thing or two about the Rules. He knew exactly what should be done, not only to preserve his own comfort, but also not to rouse the passions of the Rules of Golf Committee. But how to get his message across to those confounded females?

Then it struck him. It was as if a light bulb had suddenly been given the juice and blazed to life above his head. He'd listen to the possible solutions to the dispute and hiss – or shake or wiggle or do something nasty – if the players were wrong.

First one of the women decided he was a loose impediment, which he most certainly was not. Offended, he scowled, shook his tail and swayed back and forth like a cobra in the throes of an exotic trance cast by an Indian fakir. They shrieked and clung to one another in terror, as colour drained from their faces and blood sought safer regions of the anatomy. They stared spellbound, unable to move.

Suddenly the rattler changed his motion. No longer did he move menacingly: rather his head began to move gently from side to side, as if saying 'No'.

After a moment the ladies broke from their hypnotic state, their eyes focused, and their blood, sensing that all was safe after all, crept cautiously back to its accustomed reaches.

'Why, I believe that dear little thing is telling us he's not a loose impediment,' one startled lovely said to the other.

'Do you think that's possible?' the other asked.

'Let's find out,' the first said. Looking the rattler squarely in the eye, she posed the question. 'Are you a loose impediment, dear?'

Blushing modestly at the endearing term, the rattler shook his head.

'Amazing!' the second cupcake gasped. 'A rattlesnake who knows the Rules.'

The snake, his face awash with a smile of beatitude, nodded his head, and with a twitch of his brow suggested they continue the interrogation.

'If you're not a loose impediment,' commented the owner of the ball that had caused all the ruckus, 'then maybe you're an obstruction?'

Again the rattler shook his head negatory at this unsettling suggestion. Unlike a loose impediment, an obstruction can be lifted with disdain and cast out of the bunker like an old beer can. He was apalled that he could be considered a candidate for such cavalier treatment. And he thought they were getting along so well.

'Well then, I suppose you must be an outside agency?' one said.

Grinning hugely, he agreed and made the proper notion to indicate that now they had the message.

'But,' one said, frowning, 'you're a dangerous outside agency, aren't you?'

Much as it pained him, he had to agree, and so he bared his fangs and, with the speed of light lunged towards them. Not very close, mind you; he wouldn't think of hurting anyone. He was just getting his message across.

It was understood, of course.

What then to do, they wondered?

From their deep frowns, he could see they were puzzled. Oh well, he thought, there's only one thing to do. Uncoiling himself slowly, lest he send them scampering back to the safety of the ladies' locker room, where he dare not enter, he slithered across the sand to a point well out of range of a fangy thrust, but still within the bunker, and tapped his nose into the sand three times, indicating that the ball should be dropped on that spot.

Then he crawled back to his original slumbering post, carefully smoothing his footprints, so to speak, wrapped himself in his coils, and settled down to watch the finish of the hole.

Catching on immediately, the woman whose waywardness had begun all this bother dropped her ball on the spot indicated and played a reasonably useful shot on to the green, but lost the hole when her opponent holed what the rattler heard them call a snake. And they moved on.

Alone again, the rattler settled down for some shuteye against the time when he would have to creep through the cactus and put food on the table. Little did he know, however, that his days of wistful bliss were coming to an end, for even now word of his remarkable powers was sweeping through the Sagebrush Country Club. His fate was sealed.

That is how Sagebrush came to have the world's most famous Rules Committee Chairman. From January through December, when first light creeps across the desert, the rattlesnake climbs on to a high rock that overlooks the thirteenth green, slips into his blue and red USGA armband, and waits for the day's business to begin. He sits in regal splendour and adjudicates disputes brought before him with all the aplomb and compassion and wisdom of P. J. Boatwright, Bobby Furber, and Judge Roy Bean. Only occasionally does he become provoked by a golfer who presses his case too strongly, and then he opens his jaws wide, curls back his upper lip and threatens to sink his fangs into one of the golfer's more sensitive parts.

But a few members know that this is just a sham. Every fourth Monday, you see, he's seen creeping across the sand to the local dispensary and donates venom for what he assumes is a worthy cause.

A word of warning. If you're ever in the vicinity of the Sagebrush Country Club and feel the urge for a stimulant, watch out for the martinis. They pack quite a wallop.

Postscript

Profound thought from Christy O'Connor
after getting soaked while playing with a member
on a rainy day at Royal Dublin:
'You know, if this wasn't my living
I wouldn't do it if you paid me.'